*Craig S. Miles*

D1790976

# The Desert Face of God

*Valley of the Valleys:
Death Valley Experiences*

&

*Desert Flowers:
A Sermonic Harvest*

## Harry R. Butman

©Harry R. Butman 1985

All rights reserved under International and Pan-American Conventions. No part of this book may be reproduced, stored in a retrieval system, or transmitted in any form or by any means, electronic, mechanical, recording or otherwise, without express written permission of the author, except for education photocopying as provided by Public Law 94-533 (Secs. 106, 107 and 108, title 17, *United States Code*.), and for brief quotations in book reviews.

**Library of Congress Cataloging in Publication Data**

ISBN 0-914598-56-2

Cover Design by Jeff Nemeroff

Photos by Barbara A. Wright

Printed in the United States of America

Published by Padre Productions
P.O. Box 1275, San Luis Obispo CA 93406

# Dedication

To Honor Pastor Emeritus Dr. Harry R. Butman
by
the Memorials Committee of the
Congregational Church of the Messiah
Los Angeles, California

## Acknowledgements

I am indebted to the Memorials Committee of the Congregational Church of the Messiah and to all those whose gifts of remembrance made this book possible. I particularly appreciate the labors of Barbara A. Wright, without whose persistence and diligence this volume would not have seen print.

*Harry R. Butman*

Other Books by Dr. Harry R. Butman

History of Randolph, Massachusetts  *1943*
Far Islands  *1954*
The Measure of the Immeasurable  *1967*
The Lord's Free People  *1968*
Serve With Gladness  *1971*
The Beecher Lectures  *1978*
The Argent Year  *1980*

# Table of Contents

Acknowledgements.................................................*vi*
Foreword..........................................................*ix*
Prologue............................................................*x*
**Part I Valley of the Valleys** ............................. 11
  1  In General ................................................. 13
  2  Death Valley .............................................. 15
  3  A Change of Interior Weather ........................ 20
  4  Panamint .................................................. 25
  5  Saline ....................................................... 28
  6  Eureka and North Death ............................... 33
  7  Racetrack.................................................. 37
  8  Greenwater ............................................... 39
  9  Butte........................................................ 42
10  Beasts, Birds, Flowers, and Rocks .................. 54
11  The Lure of the Desert ................................. 65
12  Seldom Seen Beauty..................................... 69
13  The Spice of Danger.................................... 73
14  Emptiness and Solitude................................ 78
15  God.......................................................... 85
16  For Beginners............................................ 89
**Part II Desert Flowers**.................................... 93
17  You Have to Go in Convoy ........................... 95
18  The Unconquest of Black Mountain ................ 102
19  The Beautiful and Friendly Beasts .................. 108
20  Three Dust Devils at Coyote Dry Lake ............ 116
21  A Fire, a Gun, and the High Stars................... 122
22  Short View from Skiddoo.............................. 129
23  Campfire at Greenwater: The Vanity of Human Hopes .... 136
24  Pete Aguereberry, Patron of the Arts............... 143
25  The Long, Cold Night on Mt. McDill ............... 151
26  The Mayor of Corn Springs: La Dolce Vita ....... 157
Epilogue ......................................................... 164
Selected References .......................................... 166

DEATH VALLEY

# Foreword

I am going to write about the desert and about a particular part of that great global reality. Some of what I say will be repetitious, since I have spoken and written much about the Mojave, but if William Blake could rewrite and rewrite his couplets and songs, I see no reason why I should be denied the privilege. After sketching the background of the world's deserts, I shall focus upon eight in America, Death Valley, the famous queen of them all, and her attendant ladies—Panamint, Saline, Eureka, North Death, Racetrack, Greenwater, and Butte. Part of this treatise will be narrative, part philosophical, and part theological. It will have a trace of mysticism. My reason for writing is that I want to share the richness and power of the desert experience as I have felt it and perhaps induce others to venture into the outback and see and know for themselves what I shall praise in inadequate words. I am no longer an active preacher, but old habits are hard to break, so I will choose a text, the verse which describes John the Baptist: *"Vox clamatis in deserto"*—"a voice of one calling in the desert" (Matthew 3:3).

# Prologue

The desert is a tremendous physical fact; one seventh of the earth's surface—eight million square miles—is desert. It is also a tremendous spiritual fact: three great world religions—Judaism, Christianity, and Islam—are desert born. When Terah, father of Abraham, went out of Ur of the Chaldees, he began the clan migration that skirted the edge of the immense Arabian desert and came into Canaan. On a mountain slope in the Sinai Desert the holy Name was revealed to Moses; on that same mountain the Ten Words were given him, and from oasis to oasis across that harsh wilderness for forty years he led his rebellious brickyard gang until they were ready to enter the Promised Land. John the Baptist was a voice crying in the desert; Jesus began his ministry with a forty day desert battle with Satan: into the desert he went to pray when his soul was thirsty for God. Muhammad, brooding by night in a desert cave near Mecca, heard a voice naming him the prophet of Allah, and by the power of that hearing he unified the feuding wilderness tribes and made them a force that captured Jerusalem and was for centuries the terror of Europe.

The American pulpit is unaware of the reality of the desert—its spatial immensity, hinting of infinity; the multiplicity and tenacity of its life forms, tribute to the Creator's imagination; its walls of everlasting hills, its nonsensuous austerity—one face of God. This book is an attempt to reap a sermonic harvest from personal desert experiences. As far as I know these discourses are a new genre; they are desert flowers with their special colors and fragrances.

# I
# Valley of the Valleys

Remember,
You are made in the image of God.
And with a curious proud humility
You may lawfully stand in the presence of the glories of creation,
And say to the dark magnitudes of mountains at night
And the blazonry of great stars above them,
"You are the work of God's fingers,
His craftsmanship,
His incredible carpentry and manufacture.
But I am his child."

*—Harry R. Butman, October 28, 1979.*

# 1
# In General

The desert, like the ocean, is an immense physical fact of the planet earth. Geographer Wladimir Köppen has defined a desert as an area with less than ten inches of rain annually. Some deserts have far less than that, of course; the average in Death Valley is 1.65 inches and in places in the Empty Quarter in Saudi Arabia twenty-five years have passed with no measurable rainfall. These vast arid areas lie astraddle the Tropics of Cancer and Capricorn. Biggest of all is the Sahara, that enormous expanse of the earth's surface, watered on its eastern edge by the Nile; three million square miles inhabited time out of mind by little bands of nomads who clustered and grazed around its few and widely spaced oases. The Sahara was temporarily conquered when the Third Augusta Legion of Rome went into Libya, and by organization, discipline, patience, and a master-race mentality, cultivated the northern Sahara and made it the bread basket of the Empire. Modern tribes still use the deep stone wells the Romans built. Next largest is the Arabian Desert, a million square miles of sand, with a desert within a desert, the enormous and desolate Rub al Khali, the Empty Quarter. The Gobi in Central Asia is 500,000 square miles in extent. But almost matching it in size is the North American Desert—the Great Basin and the Sonoran Desert, with our familiar Mojave as a transition area. Large also are the Patagonian Desert in Argentina and the Atacama of the Andean coast. Sizable likewise are the Thar of India (I'm not lisping in print, I don't mean the Star of India, that's a ship) and the Takla Makan of China, adjacent to the Gobi. I name two others which have long held a charm for me—the Kalahari of South Africa and the great Australian desert which comprises forty-four per cent of that continent's surface. By way of comparison, only five per cent of the North American Continent is desert. It is a source of regret to me that when I was in Africa some seventeen years ago, I couldn't take advantage of an invitation which Don Roberts of Covenant Presbyterian Church in Westchester might have arranged for me with an Anglican missionary friend who was posted near the Kalahari, a waste well told of by Laurens van der Post in his fine book, *The Heart of the Hunter*. I have long wanted to travel to Alice Springs in the great outback of the Australian bush. It seems unlikely now that I will.

# 2

# Death Valley

I move nearer home and speak of a place many of you have seen, and if you have not, you should see that austerely splendid place before you die. The literature on Death Valley is extensive, and the color photos of the masters of the lens who have made photographic books will give you some idea of the chromatic splendor of this National Monument. Stanley W. Paher's two volumes on Death Valley Ghost Towns is a particularly fine example of informative text and old photos. I'm not going to say much about Death Valley. The illustrated map issued by the Automobile Club of Southern California provides a gazeteer of beauty spots, accommodations, and hazards, and is such a complete piece of work that I need say little about this justly famous place of visitation.

From January till May Death Valley is ideal for touring, with places to stay ranging from the dusty and uninspiring campground at Stovepipe Wells to posh Furnance Creek Inn where you can pay plenty for Sybaritic luxury in the midst of the consistently hottest place in the world. Azizia, a town in Libya, once registered the record, 136.4 degrees in the shade, but Death Valley's 1919 top air temperature, 134 degrees, is close, and the ground temperature of Death Valley is higher than any other place on the globe. In 1972, there was a ground reading of 201 degrees. Summer temperature are often in the high 120s, and all-in-all, it's a nice place to stay away from in summer months.

But the winter weather is often halcyon, and the touring is very pleasant. (I once spent a night there, however, when the glass was down to 17 degrees, and the snow level dropped to 2000 feet, which made mile-high Towne's Pass a possible sticking point.) Visit the known and glamorous places—Scotty's Castle, that big, beautiful Spanish house wealthy Albert Johnson built as a winter home, and which his private clown, Death Valley Scotty, persuaded the gullible was his personal property —and the fine Museum at Furnace Creek. Dante's View is a first-time must. If the weather is clear you can look almost straight down and see the lowest spot in the United States, Badwater, 282 feet below sea level, while ninety miles away is the highest peak in the Lower Forty-Eight States, Mt. Whitney, soaring to 14,501 feet.

But this is no travel guide to Death Valley. I'm merely going to tell of one personal experience. The publisher of my book *Serve With Gladness* cut it out of the manuscript because he feared it would damage my reputation for sobriety and sanity. But here it is. Some twenty-odd years ago my wife and I made a pilgrimage to the grave of Shorty Harris, which lies on the Westside Road. Shorty was a gold-finder extraordinary, and his Bullfrog Mine and his World Beater were among the classic gold strikes. We cruised down the dusty Westside Road one late spring day, until we came to the place by the roadside where stood a little monument, cement base and bronze plaque mounted on a slab of granite. It was paid for, I believe, by a chapter of the Sons of the Golden West, and erected by the Civilian Conservation Corps in the early 1930s. We read the eloquent epitaph; Shorty wrote his own.

> Write me down as a one-jackass, single-blanket prospector, and bury me beside my comrade Frank Dayton, in the Valley we both loved.

Only those who know the icy chill of the desert night can appreciate Shorty's boast that he could survive with one blanket. And the great

*Graves of Shorty Harris and Frank Dayton*

spaces and the widely separated waterholes would cause a lesser man to have two or three burros in his train. We gazed in silent appreciation, and I said, "Let's pour a drink on his grave. He must be thirsty. Get out the bottle of sherry."

My wife stared at me in disgust. "Sherry!" she snorted. "Sherry for an old hard-bitten desert rat? He'd laugh you to scorn."

"Well, I don't feel like wasting good Scotch on the ground," I said.

"If you're that tight," Jennette said tartly, "he can have my share."

So with due solemnity we poured a generous libation of Ballentines on the dry earth by the marker. It was now hot, windless noon, and we decided to sleep for a while. We had a Studebaker with front seats that would go all the way down, and so, in the scant shade of the mesquite bush, we fell asleep.

We were jarred awake by a loud crashing sound. "It must be a car going by," I said. I got out to look. There was no sign of dust north or south along the long, empty road. Perplexed, we resumed our nap. As we were about to leave I decided to take a last look at Shorty's grave. I stood amazed at what I saw. The heavy granite marker had been knocked over and lay on the ground beside the cement base.

"Jennette," I cried, "come here." She came and looked, and then said awestruck, "It was Shorty."

Gooseflesh stiffened the hair on my arms. I said, "Do you know what Shorty sold the Bullfrog Mine for? One thousand dollars and a barrel of whiskey."

Now in order to get the full impact of this happening you need to know a bit of Greek mythology and one of the presumptions of psychic investigation. The ancient Greeks believed that the dead existed in a dark underground place: it wasn't hell; there was no torment. They had drunk from the stream Lethe and lived without pain in gray forgetfulness. But if you wanted to talk with one of them you could conjure him up by sacrificing an ox on his grave, for the life-blood of the beast, seeping down, would give the departed spirit force and shape enough to be briefly seen and heard. Also it is a truism of those who seek to deal with discarnates who have crossed over that while the wise go on toward a source of light, the stupid or dull cling to the familiar place where they lived in the flesh. These are "earthbound spirits." Be it considered then, that Shorty Harris was not too bright; his foolish sales and sprees following big strikes are evidence of that. After death he might well stay on in the Valley that he loved. Consider further that he had an obsessive craving for alcohol. For thirty years he had lain parched in his lonely grave. Then, miraculously, down through the dust comes trickling such liquor as he may never have tasted in the flesh. What a resultant explosion of psychic force! What a manifestation surpassing the appearances of dead Greek heroes given substance by ox blood! This powerful psychic surge overturned the grave stone with a great noise.

Lest this last seem to be an impossible quantity of psycho-kenetic energy, I bid you remember the well-authenticated case of a family tomb in one of the West Indies (Martinique, it might be; memory fails, and I have no book of reference at hand) in which, at the time of each new interment, great nine hundred pound leaden caskets were found in random disarray, standing on end or upside down, and all this taking place in a locked tomb, without help of hand of flesh. The family was so troubled by this that they permanently sealed the tomb, and what now takes place by way of psychic detonation no man knows.

Accept this tale or not; I have a great indifference to those who turn up their noses at psychic phenomena. In this case we were there, they weren't, and their arbitrary dictim of impossibility does not impress me. The most sensible thing ever said on the matter by an intellectual skeptic was spoken by G. K. Chesterton who, when asked, "Do you believe in ghosts?" answered, "No, but I'm afraid of them." Anyway, I finished this yarn in the deleted manuscript of my book with a long, carefully crafted sentence telling of poor Scotty's wraith, enduring the blazing summer noons of the hottest place on earth year after arid year, hoping that some kind traveller would once more bless him with a potent libation.

The thought troubled me, so one day about ten years later, I went back alone to Shorty's grave, with full flask, and a readiness to do a deed of mercy. But as I drove south along the Westside Road I saw the smoke of a great burning ahead of me. I found that they were cutting down the mesquite growth and that the bronze marker had been moved and placed on a bigger monument of desert stones. The young ranger who was tending the burning of the trees knew nothing of the original site. So, alas, the exact place of Scotty's burial is not known, at least by me, and I cannot do him a further wild kindness.

Here I say a word about what has become my favorite stretch of dirt —the Amargosa River road. If you would enter Death Valley by an adventurous route, get off I 15 at Baker and drive north on State 127. It's a lonesome stretch, hard surface, easy going, but totally houseless, passing through two dry lakes, Silver and Silurian, with the Avawatz Mountains off to the left. Thirty miles out from Baker you will come to Wade's Exit, named for a pioneer who escaped from Death Valley with his family by this way. Turn left and go along the dirt road which follows the Amargosa River, dry most of the time. The Amargosa road is like a fickle and beautiful woman, full of charm and peril. The road is smoothly graded until you reach the junction of the trail that leads to Owl Hole Spring. There, at the entrance to Death Valley National Monument, you will be confronted with a series of signs bearing grim warnings: "Rough Road," "This road not patrolled daily," "Difficult river crossing twelve miles ahead," and a pictograph of a jeep.

I liken the road to a sexy and dangerous woman because at times it offers sheer beauty—emptiness, clean sky, and green mesquite stretching to the ever-changing panorama of the mountain walls of the great wash. But the road is not constant. My most recent passage was occasioned by the fact that southbound, we had run out of daylight, and there was no campground on pavement for over a hundred miles. With trepidation, since there had been severe rains a few days before, I opted for risking the river road and spending the night at some convenient pulloff. My concern was sharpened by a new sign—"Deep Sand." A few miles south we suddenly saw the reality of the warning. Great dangerous drifts of the yellow peril lay across the road. I dropped into second gear, hit the gas as hard as I dared, and ploughed through, lurching and slewing, but not stopping. This is an example of the shifting nature of this road: on five previous trips this stretch was perfectly passable, no least trace of sand.

But for all its treachery, I like this road, not only because it is the loneliest dirt in Death Valley, but because of the impromptu camps made by its sides. Two safaris, flood-stopped and night-caught, pulled off on the empty hardpan at the crossing and made merry by campfire while the hot winds howled, drying the river without causing a sand storm. But the latest camp was the best. As night deepened and Orion and the Bull glittered, we sat by the tiny fire eating. Suddenly a white shadow slid along the edge of the light—a kit fox, lured by the smell of broiling meat. We tossed him a bit of steak; he daringly darted, grabbed, and disappeared into the bush. He reappeared; we made him come nearer this time, and the ravenous hunger all wild creatures incessantly know overcame his fear. Closer and closer he came, till at last he took bits of cold cuts from the toe of my boot. It was fascinating to watch him circling ghost-like in the shadows and coming nearer, finally putting his tiny catlike feet on top of the cooler, sniffing for a goodie, and bringing his long delicate nose within a few feet of the fire. After a while he did not dash in and out, but would stay in the firelight so we could see his great inquisitive eyes, long ears, graceful little body and plumed tail. He was not as big as a house cat. He was a sweet rare vision of fugitive grace and loveliness, one of the unexpected rewards of being in the outback by night.

# 3

# A Change of Interior Weather

This is all I am going to say about Death Valley, but before I go on to talk about things in the circling seven, I must do an autobiographical sketch and tell of a change in my own spirit. I have in my later years become something of a desert rat, and this represents a radical alteration in my outdoor orientation. I come of seafaring folk. Since Jeremiah Butman helped found the town of Beverly, Massachusetts, in 1638, my people have dwelt in seaport towns—Manchester, Ipswich, Essex, Rockport. In my infancy I was subject to the lure of the water. Indeed, my earliest clear memory was walking out on the flats at Dane Street Beach in Beverly (I couldn't have been much more than three years old at the time) and being fascinated by a giant crab in a tidal pool near the deep and dangerous channel. As a boy I rowed a dory of my grandfather's making around the coves of the Bass and Danvers Rivers and historic Salem Harbor. My father and I once rowed up the Danvers River to drink from a spring which had quenched rambling Nathaniel Hawthorne's thirst.

As a mature man (although a novice to sail), I sailed a series of half-decked sloops around Vineyard and Nantucket Sounds, thrice in peril of my life. Once, while running before a smoky sou'wester on returning from Cuttyhunk with the tall pursuing combers rising evilly astern, I put my wife's life in hazard. In the foolish traversing the West Cho Rip in a half-gale I imperiled my brother's life, and in attempting to get off lonely Muskeget Island in a heavy blow, that of my son. I have also cruised the scenic waters of Penobscot Bay and the marvelous fiords of the Pacific Northwest—the San Juan Islands, the Straits of Georgia, and the tremendous tides of British Columbia. I loved it all, and so it came as something of a surprise both to myself and to those who knew me, when suddenly, I fell out of love with the sea and became a devotee of the desert. This is how it happened.

For several years after coming to California, when I fell into a daytime reverie I would often picture the familiar waters of my childhood and maturity, both in their fierce and benign aspects. And whenever sleep was slow in coming at night, I would start to construct a boat in my mind. The models were many, but they were mentally built from transom to stem, from keel to masthead, piece by piece and nail by nail, until the weary wits refused to carry any more detail, and I would subside into somnolence. My unconscious loved the water. But one Sunday morning as I sat in the Edgartown Church where I was ordained, listening to the minister drone interminably through a plethora of announcements, suddenly, uninvited, there appeared in my mind's eye a desert vista— a long, tan valley stretching endlessly into the blue of the distance, with brown and black buttes standing like steadfast sentinels. It was an unsought interior change, a psychic shift; not conscious, not of the will. The prevailing winds of my interior life turned around; the compass course of my spirit directed me to the desert rather than to the ocean. Someone once asked me how I could make the drastic shift, and I said, "Well, the desert and the sea aren't all that different. They're both big and flat, and they'll kill you if you aren't careful." There was more to it than that, as I shall later tell, but that's how the business started.

There was, however, a mechanical analogy which made the transition easier for me to understand. I had long resolved, in my younger days, that if by any unlikely chance affluence ever came, I would buy a little gaff-rigged cruising sloop, slow but seaworthy, in which I could make voyages not possible in my half-decked boats. Now if the camel can be called a ship of the desert, I see no reason why a pickup truck may not be called a land yacht. By truck I have had many cruises to desert places and cast anchor for the night in lonely canyon or flat thick with Joshua trees. By truck I have gone to isolated mountain brooks and ghost towns, and bivouacked (pistol under pillow), with the stars burning overhead and the alluring emptiness of the wilderness all around me.

Now before I take you on safari, or move you to make your own desert passages, let me speak a word about transportation. In the first place, while four-wheel-drive vehicles (hereafter called 4WD), are the best, you don't actually need one to reach many remote and lonely places. Indeed, there is a danger for the novice and even the seasoned driver in the extended mobility of the 4WD vehicle; it tempts you to go on and on until you reach the place where you can't go on, and perhaps can't even turn around to go back.

"A 4WD just means you'll get stuck further in," a veteran back country driver once morosely advised me.

Incidentally, the term "off-road vehicle" is lightly used, and the popular magazines devoted to desert driving aren't accurately named. For one thing, the Forestry Service and the Bureau of Land Management are very negative about trucks leaving the roads and trails and going cross-country where no track exists. What is generally meant by an "off-road vehicle" is actually an "off-pavement vehicle." Many, though of course not all, of the trips I shall describe could have been made by a passenger car of reasonable ground clearance, well-tuned, with good tires, wisely driven.

The truck that got me out into the back country was a small Datsun two-wheel-drive, which means that actually only one wheel delivered power. He was a jaunty orange fellow, with a camper top my wife and son picked up as a fine bargain. I personalize and name my cars, perhaps a carry-over from sailing days. The old Vineyard boatmen considered that it was very back luck to have a boat without a name. This anonymity, they somehow reasoned, was an insult to the sea, and the disfavor of the sea was something to be avoided. I called him "The Corporal" at first, but after a noble deed in Waucoba Pass which I shall later narrate, he got a field promotion and is now "The Sergeant." He is an incredibly tough little truck, and twice came down the seven dry falls of Goler Wash, passages which we had no right to expect of him. I remember him with affection, and I recall one occasion when, as silly as it sounds, he inspired me to do something I might not have done otherwise. It was on a bright Sunday morning. I had gone up the Big Pine road to North Death Valley and had reached a place where Little Sand Spring Trail strikes northeast to Oriental Wash and Gold Point, Nevada. Ahead lay the Last Chance Range. I had never been through there and I was afraid of it. I looked at the Sergeant. Mrs. Butman had put his name on the cab in irridescent letters and I swear that they sparkled in the morning sun with an extra vividness and by this glister the Sergeant said, "Come on; we can make it." I heeded the Sergeant's brave counsel and had a fine, if tough, trip past Crankcase Junction and on into Cowhorn Valley.

But I wanted something a little bigger and so I sold him to my son and bought my present vehicle, "Excelsior"—"upward and onward." He is a Plymouth Arrow sport truck with the then biggest engine available—a potent 2.6 Mitsubishi. (There has been a clamor of late against buying Japanese cars. The reason so many of us have done so is that the Japanese adopted our Puritan work ethic and turned out machines of high quality. Detroit—labor and management both—has now started to correct its sloppy workmanship and produce cars that are well-made.) Excelsior is not strictly stock any more; he's been modified for the outback. Oversize tires to begin with; knobby all-terrains on the rear wheels and big six-ply truck tires on the front. Smooth, narrow, freeway rubber is not the stuff for steep grades, mud, sand, and rocks. At a cost considerably greater than I paid for my first new car, I had installed a limited slip differential which makes both rear wheels provide driving power. This gear and these tires double my traction in bad going and make full use of the abundant torque my tuned engine provides. I have also an aluminum skid plate in front to keep sharp rocks from performing heavy surgery on my motor pan.

*Titus Canyon*

In the cab I have a shovel, water containers, and a device which enables me to pump up my tires from the engine if I have to soften them to traverse deep sand. I have a compass and an altimeter, and behind the seat a pretty complete tool kit. My camper is an Alaskan which rides in a low position, but which can be pumped up to give six feet of headroom in camp. It isn't very streamlined, and it's so heavy that I have had to install gas shocks and larger helper springs in the rear. But with its foam-rubber bunks, propane stove, and table, it can be comfortable on a cold, snowy night in the mountains. In its lockers are suits of thermal underwear, rain gear, tow rope, extra oils of divers sorts, and many odd bits of equipment and clothing. I can mount two five-gallon jerry cans of gas, which give me a cruising range of a bit over 500 miles. All recreational vehicles are compromises between comfort and mobility; in terms of comfort you can go down from a motor home to a dune buggy. My rig has considerable comfort, and while Excelsior is not the match of a 4WD in getting into bad places, he will take me as far in as I ought to go. He isn't the ultimate bad road machine, but he's more car than I am driver. He is powerful and dependable. I am happy with him. He has given me many exciting and pleasant hours.

A few words should be said about camping sites. Death Valley has nine, ranging from campgrounds with no shade or water and with primitive facilities, for which no fee is charged, to others with shade, tables, toilets, and showers. For these there is a fee and senior citizens with Golden Age passports are charged half-price. There are no formal campgrounds in the seven surrounding valleys, and you must simply pull off the road in a good spot, taking care that the ground is hard enough to ensure getting back onto the road in the morning. There are some Park Service taboos, however. For example, no overnight camping is allowed in Race Track Valley, or in areas restricted to day camping. In the back country you must be a mile away from the road (more honored in the breach than in the observance) and at least five miles from a campground. You must stay at least a quarter of a mile away from any source of water; camping closer frightens the wild life. Pets are not permitted on the trails. Respect the private property in the Monument, watch for snakes, and stay away from mineshafts. What you pack in, you should carry out: don't leave litter. The rule, "Take nothing but pictures, leave nothing but footprints," is a good one. More details on these matters can be found in brochures available at any Ranger station.

# 4

# Panamint

Get into the cab with me now and we'll begin our safari through the seven virtually unvisited valleys. This essay won't be the match of "A Week on the Concord and Merrimack" because I'm not the writer Thoreau was, but the scenery we will see and the distance we will cover would have stunned Yankee Henry. (After all, he camped in his backyard; Walden Pond was a mile-and-a-half from home, and his sister could walk out to bring him freshly baked cookies.)

    The first valley is Panamint, a haunted and storied place. I got the idea of its ghostliness both from Russ Leadabrand and experience. His stories in *Westways* got me started on back country driving, and somewhere he says that Panamint is haunted, and that others can corroborate his feelings. There is no place, he claims, where one has a stronger sense of "the Old Ones" than in great, gray Panamint. It has a feel; perhaps the ghosts of the ancient Indians who eked out an existence here, perhaps from the wraiths of the prospectors who once made crumbled Ballarat a busy trading center, or perhaps Seldom Seen Slim still lingers where he lived in the flesh.

    The initial glimpse of Panamint is dramatic. As you drive northward from Trona, a company town on Searles Dry Lake—where the Kerr-Magee Company takes more money from the salts of that ancient sea than the prospectors ever found in gold—you climb over a ridge and there, instantly, breathtakingly, is the whole long lonely expanse. At the crest of the hill you can see forty miles to the north where the dunes are golden, and another thirty miles into the hazy blue south where the valley runs into the Naval Weapons Center. (It has always seemed odd to me that the Navy, a seafaring operation, should claim hundreds of thousands of acres of the dryest land on the continent.) To your right is the barren Panamint Range, brown, black, ochre, and if it be winter or spring, tall Telescope Peak, the 11,049 foot sentinel of Death Valley, will have a wide silver crown. The valley is not quite uninhabited. There is a flourishing onyx mine (curiously, an onyx mine is not a shaft, but a hilltop of incredibly variegated rock) and a small restaurant at Panamint Springs on Route 190. There are a few folk at Indian Ranch reservation just where the paved road swings northeast into Wildrose Canyon.

But Ballarat itself is dead, for the present, at least. A few years ago a woman started a store, but it petered out. In the late Sixties, Panamint Valley had fleeting fame. A group of hippies planned an Easter sunrise celebration, at which they expected some 500,000 people to gather, Woodstock-style, to hail the rising sun with heathen rites. It was sheer idiocy, of course. There was no water and no accommodations. Quite a number did assemble, some ten thousand, it was estimated; but the sole result was that some nature-loving hippie got stoned, let his fire get away from him, and burned half the stand of trees that had been growing south of the town for long years. Ballarat, named for the Australian gold town, has been ill-used by vandals. Twice the bronze marker at the junction of the pavement has been chisled loose and most likely sold for scrap bronze. The original name of the town was Post Office Springs, and in the days when prospectors were inching through the many canyons of the towering Panamint Range, on Saturday night it was a wild and rowdy place.

I have vivid memories of Panamint Valley; I first saw it nearly thirty years ago crossing it on the Towne's Pass Road. But in later years the contact has been closer. Once, far at the south end, we lost the slave cylinder of our Datsun on the rocks of the dry falls of Goler Wash, where the Charles Manson family hid out. Twice we have tried to get to Panamint City, a high-elevation ghost town which once produced much silver. Once we were stopped by an improbable event, a traffic jam in Surprise Canyon. A Volvo passenger car, rashly essaying the climb, was stuck, and the 4WD's out cruising on that holiday were piled up behind it. We turned around and got out. Baffled, we later took another shot at it. This time, slogging upward through the snow-melt brook that flowed along the canyon floor, we lost a tire on the jagged rocks. I have not tried it since.

But I have oddly durable memories of a night in Panamint Valley. I had driven as far as I could above Ballarat to the mouth of Pleasant Canyon and then proceeded on foot. It was off this canyon that Shorty Harris found the rich World Beater mine. Two strange things happened on my walk in Pleasant Canyon; rusty, wrecked, and immovably caught in the mud-and-rock wash of many years ago, were two Fords, vintage Forties, trapped, stuck beyond salvaging. A little later on the canyon, harsh and bare, suddenly became an Eden-like place of running water, green trees, and small singing yellow birds. I came down the slope to where my car was waiting, just as the red sun touched the top of Wild Horse Mesa across the Valley. I sat in my Monte Carlo (this was before the days of my trucks) and drank Rusty Nails (Scotch and Drambuie in equal parts) until it was time to get out my sleeping bag and bed down for the night. I was, I fear, very enScotched. At first I laid my bag into the wind, which was now nearly a gale, and only after great effort put it the other way so that my feet were into the wild gusting. Cowboys, I have read, used to ring their sleeping place with a horsehair lariat, for rattlers, they maintained, would not crawl into the blankets of a sleeper thus guarded. I used a ring of insect repellent. It was a strange sleepless night with many wild fancies and fantasies, and I remember it with clarity and delight.

For more than a decade those perpetually stuck Fords have haunted me. I made three unavailing trips seeking them; one in my son's Jeep. We had to turn back after losing the trail. The second time I hunted vainly for the canyon road. The third time I found it, but it was too late in the day to walk. Recently I tried again. I thought I had found it, but it was a new mining road that branched off and climbed what must have been at least a 25 per cent grade, perhaps 30 per cent. I would walk ahead seeking turnouts, lest a crumbling lip leave us with the unpleasant necessity of backing down, a dangerous process. The truck was in low and the pedal was to the metal. At the trail head I walked a way and looked down to see the canyon, deep, narrow, black, but with the tree-bordered road awash. To my surprise, I saw a black 4WD steaming bravely upstream, bow-wave white. It disappeared under the lip of the canyon, and then I heard the whine of the motor and the snarl of wheels spinning in gravel, cut engine, quiet. A bit later the engine came on again with a long series of snarling surges. Then silence. Stuck. There was nothing we could do to help; our rig would never get us up to their sticking place. I did find the right turn-off on the trip down—first gear against compression, the brakes on hard—and I will drive up there some day and try it on foot again.

# 5

# Saline

Saline Valley first piqued my curiosity some quarter of a century ago when I looked over a map of California and saw a route which ran for 87 miles without a town. It must be the loneliest road in the state, I thought; sometime I will drive it. I did not get around to doing it until 1975, when, on a grayish December day, my son Jack and I turned off State Route 190 and started up the wide and well-paved road into Saline Valley, a condition that lasts until the junction with the San Lucas Canyon road, where it becomes good dirt and climbs toward Hunter Mountain.

San Lucas Canyon is worth a parenthetical comment. Several years later, intrigued by the smooth well-graded dirt road that led to it, I made a special trip of exploration. I later learned that this good condition was due to the attention given it by the owners of the Bonham Talc mine, whose big trucks regularly make the run. I went on up, with the going worsening a bit, looking for a place to spend the night. I decided to turn back to the last place I recalled being able to get off the road. It was Lee Flat, a thick grove of Joshua trees. I cranked up my camper and set out for a walk. The rich slow fire of sunset was gorgeous over the Inyo Range, and I pushed on much farther than was wise. When I turned back to face the east, the distant Argus Range was black against the shine of the first stars. It was a moonless night and the going was rough. To keep my mind off my growing fatigue, as I walked I worked out what I call the doctrine of the two dependencies. I was, I concluded, first dependent on man; in this case the Japanese craftsmen who had built an honest truck that would not fail and leave me far from help in the back country. And as I stumbled along in the dark on the uncertain footing, I worried about what would happen if I broke an ankle. I could not truly rely upon my failing muscles and sinews. My second dependency, therefore, was upon God, whom I trusted to guide and protect me in all my goings. So I wearily plodded along, very glad when the starshine showed the white glimmer of my truck through the Joshua trees.

I later took a safari there. We went up to the mines at seven thousand feet, looked wistfully at a turn-off which might have been the jeep trail to the crest of the Inyo Range and Cerro Gordo, that mountain once marvelously rich in silver. But on the way back to Lee Flat we were hit with a surprise October snow storm; the wind was high and the flakes thick. We huddled in my camper for a cocktail hour; myself, four people, and a handsome Irish setter. The night was bitterly cold, and in the morning poor Orion, a creature of hot, smoggy Los Angeles, one who had never seen snow before, stood shivering in the icy dawn, an incongruous red handkerchief about his neck, wondering what this white stuff was that clung to his cold feet.

But back to the first trip. It was late in the afternoon when Jack and I turned north down Grapevine Canyon into Saline Valley, and as we went up the long lonesome road we looked in vain for a good place to spend the night. There was a single light in the mine at Willow Creek, but we wanted solitude and we pressed on towards Jackass Flat. But as we gained altitude the darkness deepened, the wind howled louder, and the cold intensified, so we turned back and found a little gully out of the wind, not far from Willow Creek. Jack got the Coleman lantern going and started supper while I went out for a walk. The clouds which had been purple to the south and to the north now covered the sky completely; not a star shone. It was so dark that I literally couldn't see where I was stepping, so I stumbled back to the camper. As we sat inside the shell, out of the wind, we saw, to our surprise and concern, the lights of a truck coming down the gulch toward us. We got out our guns; out there, you never know.

But nothing threatening appeared in the circle of light. The truck was a big, new 4WD Ford; the driver was a young man, and neither he nor his young wife left the safety of the cab. He asked, "Are we in Death Valley?"

We stared at each other. If he could have levitated his rig over the Cottonwood Mountains, he was perhaps forty miles from Stovepipe Wells. But by the nearest road it was at least double that.

"No," I told him. "You're in Saline Valley. Let me show you on your map."

"I haven't got a map," he said.

Our glances at each other said wordlessly that this couldn't be real.

Who would come out into the desert in the night without a map? His fine new machine was that of a novice; nobody with any sense would be out here mapless. "Will you have a drink?" Jack asked.

He looked at his wife, got an almost imperceptible negative and said, "No, thanks." From this small evidence we deduced that they were teetotalers, and we have ever after referred to the spot, perhaps inaccurately, as Lost Mormon Camp. We couldn't give him our one map, but on a scrap of paper we pencilled the nearest way out—back up Grapevine Canyon to Route 190, and east to Panamint Springs where there was then a service station. He had plenty of gas, which showed some common sense. He thanked us, and the truck went lurching away. We didn't worry about them. There was no reason why he could not have easily made it back to a place of habitation.

We put our planks in place across the shell at tonneau level, laid down the foam rubber pads and crawled into our sleeping bags. You couldn't sit up, and it was hard to get out. Once in, you were there to stay, and the winter nights are long. This one was also cold, and the frost was thick on the glass. We rejoiced that we had come back to a lower altitude and some shelter.

In the morning, stiff, half-paralyzed with cold, we fell out of the back end of the camper and miserably endured until the cup of hot coffee was ready. That first cup of strong, steaming brew, warming the chilled fingers as well as the shivering body, is one of the blessed experiences in the winter outback. A couple of cups down the hatch and you begin to think that you will live after all, and that life might yet prove worth living. As we bounced up the long, rough climb out of the valley, we saw a lovely sight. In the dusk of the previous evening we had seen strange black shadows beside the road; morning light showed them to be a herd of burros; it was in truth Jackass Flats. Now I had always considered mules to be drab beasts of burden. But these were splendid creatures, fur of lustrous gray and glossy black, with great gorgeous eyes. They were not afraid of us, for this was before the time when the Forestry Department decided that the descendants of the burros abandoned by prospectors had multiplied to such an extent that they were over-grazing the scant vegetation, and indigenous animals, the big horn sheep especially, were threatened with extinction by the numerous and aggressive burros. They are systematically shot from time to time, and these days it is harder to get near them.

On a later safari a number of us saw huge herds of burros in Butte Valley; we were told that the burro population of that small but well-watered vale was over three hundred. We could see perhaps seventy-five at one time. A few days later I told this to a tall, blonde Park Ranger (there's lots of females in the business now), and she said, "Why, just the other day we were over there in a helicopter looking for them and we didn't see one." I said, "Miss, burros aren't stupid. Don't you think that they know by now what the coming of a helicopter means?" She smiled wanly. Incidentally, for the sake of those who have wondered about the various names of this general class of fauna, I will now tabulate them for you.

The general term is ass, which is any of several hoofed animals of the genus Equus; it is closely related to horses and zebras. A jackass is a male ass. A mule is a sterile hybrid of a male ass and a female horse. They are very intelligent, strong, and tough. A hinny is a hybrid offspring of a male horse and a female ass. The donkey is a domesticated ass. A burro is a small donkey, especially one used as a pack animal. I have read that the onager, the wild ass of Central Asia, is large and handsome. This information is probably more than you care to know, but I put it in to help myself remember it. I'm always getting the types mixed up.

We were impressed with the dozen or fifteen burros, beauties free and proud in the cold winter wind. In fact I wrote a sermon about them called "The Beautiful and Friendly Beasts" (p. 108), which is an examination of the relationships of men and animals, actual and ideal. I quote St. Francis of Assisi, and relate my own private doctrine, which is counter to Roman Catholic theology, which holds that animals have no souls. (Perhaps this is why Latins often use their beasts abominably.) My view is that animals have rudimentary souls, and can display the qualities of courage, fidelity, friendship, humor, love, and therefore may well have an immortal part which will go to an animal heaven. Or maybe ours. I believe that my Abyssinian cat, Brown Boy, is a nobler, if less intricate, creature than some humans of my acquaintance.

Now we are climbing out of Saline Valley, and the dark clouds are hiding the top of Waucoba Mountain. Suddenly we had cause to worry. Snow. I was at the wheel and flogged the poor Corporal up the steepening grade in the deepening snow. He did his best, but with me at the wheel it wasn't enough. A small drift stopped us. This was serious. It was a long way back, and we had no assurance that the upper reaches of Grapevine Canyon were clear. We couldn't be far from Waucoba Summit, I figured, so I walked on ahead to look things over. To my delight, I found that we were only about half a mile from the crest. I hurried back to tell Jack that it wasn't far.

As I went, I heard the tortured whine of the Corporal's motor revving up. I found that Jack had gotten him out of the drift and had made a couple of hundred yards up the hill. I read later that in light snow, narrow hard tires are better than wide ones; they cut down through the snow to the bare ground. I got in back and pushed. Jack skillfully twisted and slewed his way upward, and though there were a couple of spots where it was touch and go, we came to the flat top of the pass. I had no altimeter then, but it was close to 8000 feet. We were silly to go in there in winter with no chains, but this was in my novice days.

"The Corporal deserves a higher rank," I said.

"Give him a field promotion," said Jack. "Make him a sergeant major."

"No," I demurred, "that takes years to get. But he shall certainly be made a top sergeant. Get out the Scotch."

With due ceremony, we lifted the hood, and on top of the radiator cap we poured a few drops of Usequebagh. We later got him some fine shiny letters, actual master sergeant's chevrons, which he proudly wears to this day.

I have been into Saline Valley six times; I like its sweep and splendor. In the spring of 1983 our safari stopped at the junction of Hunter Mountain Road and looked down at Lake Hills, where we had spent the previous night. We had travelled a long circular route and now the north Panamint dunes lay four thousand feet below us, golden in the morning sun. (Oddly, seen from the south on the previous day, they had been blue.) We dropped down the long Grapevine Canyon road, newly graded, and finally came out on the flats, where the road was abominably washboarded. We had intended to take the ordinary route north over Waucoba Pass, but a young man in a fine off-road rig, complete with petite redheaded wife and blonde child, told us that the winter rains had made the road impassable.

We had to turn back, but we were able to visit the warm springs, some seven lumpy miles off the road. We found the Lower Spring too full of nudists, male and female, complete with beer cans, to be wholly comfortable for sedate souls like ourselves. The same sort of bathers were present at Upper Warm Spring a mile or so further on, but in lesser number. Some of us, decently garbed as became sober Congregationalists, used a vacant hot pool for a dip before turning back over the long reverse route to Mesquite Springs. We marked the rusty ruins of the old tramway towers which once transported salt over the mountains to market. On a windy spring day, with the great cloud shadows racing along the barren, precipitous, red-and-black sides of the Inyos—jagged skyline against cobalt sky and creamy, dark-bottomed clouds—Saline Valley is a place of grand viewing.

# 6
# Eureka and North Death

These are seldom visited. Indeed, many people have never heard of Eureka, and some would say that North Death is not a separate valley at all. But they are worthy of mention and each has an interesting item. I first heard of Eureka from two men in a snow-tired Datsun truck who came upon us in Waucoba Pass while the Sergeant was catching his breath after the struggle out of Saline. They had been worried about reaching the crest, for while they had the right tires, their little 1600cc motor was "down to four miles an hour in low gear." North of the pass the road winds through the spectacular curves of the Narrows and comes out on hard surface; to the west is Big Pine and to the east is Cowhorn Valley, a pleasant drive through the pines. Cowhorn is a very narrow valley, hardly more than a wide gorge. Just before the road turns south-west into the Last Chance Range, there is an intriguing jeep trail which leads into Horse Thief Canyon and on over into Nevada. I'd like to try it some time, but from the looks of the terrain, I'd want to be in convoy with a 4WD.

## Eureka

The road across Eureka Valley is as straight as a ruler and at one time had a washboarding that could not be driven comfortably at any speed; slow or fast, the bumps racked you and your truck hideously. The first time I came through Eureka Valley the wind was whistling and a tall savage sandstorm was raging between the road and the Saline Range. I was worried, for once, years ago, near White Water on the Palm Springs road, I had the windshield of my old Rover pitted in a few seconds of pebble-blast. But the sand devil kept his distance, and I turned off and went nine miles south to the base of the valley's one attraction, the dunes.

It is curious that so little is said about them. For me, they are far more impressive than the more famous dunes in Death Valley. Dunes, say the wise in such things, come in four styles—star, transverse, longitudinal, and barcane. I don't know just which one of these classifications applies to the Eureka Dunes, but they tower high. This is not their only scenic quality, however. Behind them there are magnificent geological markings—zigzag ochre and taupe stripes with white edgings that change colors as the sun westers. These vivid, sharp-angled bands stand out in dramatic contrast with the black escarpment of the Last Chance Range. The dunes themselves are more gold than silver, and it is odd that the camera fans who have taken so many shots of the far less striking dunes near Stovepipe Wells, Zabriskie Point, and Dante's View should have neglected this place of big, bold beauty. Admittedly, it is out-of-the-way on a dead-end road, but it's not that hard to reach.

For a time I had thought of having my ashes sprinkled at the base of the Eureka Dunes because of their loneliness, austerity, and seldom-seen beauty. When I told Jack this, and asked him to note it for future reference, he said mockingly, "I'll make a little on the side, Pastor, guiding pilgrims to your grave." I had previously intended to have my mortal remains scattered in a fine and lonely place in Iron Canyon in the El Pasos. (I have a good shot of the Sergeant creeping down the side-angled road into Black Mountain Wash, taken from that spot.) But I went up there for an overnight trip with Mrs. Butman, who loathed it because of the roughness and the heat, and found that far from being as remote as I thought, the distant headlights of cars coming down from Walker Pass and Rt 14, were clearly to be seen. Incidentally, my wife found only one consolation in the trip. In the morning, just before we came out of Iron Canyon, we saw a covey of baby quail—there must have been over thirty of them—scuttling up the sheer face of a cliff, herded by two anxious adult birds. We figured these two were baby sitting for a colony of quail; it seemed improbable that one pair could have that many offspring of their own.

But, to return to the Eureka Dunes, I have ruled against them as a final depository of my earthly element. I've decided on Perspiration Point, on the way to Messenger Flats, not far from Strawberry Patch, my home. The place gets its name from a monument erected by a company of Civilian Conservation Corps boys, who built the road back in the Thirties. On the cement monument are the broken fastenings and the shadowed outlines of a pick and shovel, the tools of the sweaty toilers. Like much else in back-country California, the tools have been stolen by vandals. Someone once asked me why I wanted to be buried, or scattered, in a lonely desert place. I answered that I doubted if I would be an earthbound spirit, and the depositing of the ashes was a symbolic act. Actually, I could be buried in quite an historic cemetery. In the ancient burying ground in Dedham, Massachusetts, there is a closed lot, in which only pastors of the Church of Christ in Dedman could be buried. Since I once was such a pastor, it might have been interesting to see if the old town ordinance was still operative. But I have left New England, except for fond historical and genealogical memory.

At one time the Hanging Rock Canyon Road through the Last Chance Range was abominably rough, but it has lately been graded. There are several abandoned mines along this canyon. At one place the smell of sulphur is strong, and you can pick up big yellow pieces of almost pure chemical. At one of the deserted mines, as we were prowling around a wrecked building, Jack said, "We have a visitor." Looking boldly at us was a raven, as big and glossy blue-black as those that walk about the lawns and courts of the Tower of London, though lacking the massive beak. Obviously he had been a pet, for he showed no fear. We fed him some crackers and almost had him eating out of our hands. I worried for him as we left the place; there are too many gun-fools abroad to whom all things furred or feathered are objects of a wanton wish to kill. Alas, the shacks where he perched and fluttered are now buried beneath the grading of a new road.

## North Death Valley

A geological purist might object to calling North Death Valley a separate entity, but I hold that the ridge near Grapevine Station is a division. As you go north out of Death Valley, the road at that point turns east to Scotty's Castle, and goes west to Ubehebe Crater. But just before you make that turn, a dirt road runs straight north. It is ominously signed, "No services for 78 miles," and "This road is not patrolled daily." It is villianously washboarded for a way and after about 13 miles a trail strikes northwest through Oriental Wash to the town of Gold Point. I have been to Gold Point from the Nevada side, but a knowledgeable man in a jeep warned me against tackling it from North Death Valley in a two-wheel drive; it took a good man on a big dirt bike, he said.

The trail passes Little Sand Spring, and there is a pleasant tale connected with the name. Sometime in the 1860's, after the fate of the Jayhawkers and the Bennett-Arcane parties had made Death Valley a place of terror, two young men started down from Lida Summit on a trip to prove something. They held that there was enough water in the great valley to enable a well-equipped, trailwise party to traverse the feared wasteland with relative ease. Just before they started a third young man, carrying a few boards, asked to join them. They were reluctant to take him since he had no horse, but finally assented. When they reached Little Sand Spring, he took one of his boards, got out some paint, and planted a fresh sign naming the watering place. It was his wish, he said, to make Death Valley easier for traveller and prospector. He named a number of springs, and some of them, notably Little Sand Spring, are now formal names on the maps. It is good to narrate that he got himself a steed. One night they noticed a horse with a peculiar white marking on his side, not far from camp. He let himself be captured, and it was found that the marking was the remainder of an old saddle blanket. The rider had perished, but the horse had survived and sought human company. The three mounted young men carried out their plan; they crossed Death Valley, found sufficient water every twenty miles or so, and experienced no hardship or peril.

It was because of a trail name that I took Jack through the Last Chance up the Big Pine Road to a place I had seen on an earlier trip. Just before the road swings southwest, a very bad trail heads over toward Nevada. Someone had set an old crankcase to mark the place and put up a crude sign, "Crankcase Junction," but to our annoyance, vandals had stolen both crankcase and sign for souvenirs. The next time I passed by, however, someone had made amends: a camshaft was there with a neat metal sign, so it became Camshaft Junction. But on my most recent trip I found that some back country drivers with a respect for tradition had brought not one, but two old crankcases, and posted a perforated metal sign indicating the roads to Big Pine and Gold Point. So at present things are as they ought to be.

# 7

# Racetrack

Racetrack is a small but charming valley. I have been there a number of times and for me it keeps a quality of fresh beauty. To get to it, you turn off the Big Pine road and go over to Ubehebe Crater. Turn right off the Ubehebe road on a trail that is marked for 4WDs. The road isn't bad, just gravelly and rough in parts. Some of it can be driven in fifth gear, so gentle is the grade and smooth the way. There is a long climb up the slope behind Tin Mountain, and one year, after a rainy winter, there was the biggest and most splendid growth of beavertail cactus I have ever seen, glowing magenta petals with a golden core. It is 26 miles in to Racetrack, and you have to come back the same way if you are in anything less mobile than a jeep.

There are two other ways out, however, and the first of them is to be found where the Lost Burro Gap trail branches off to climb the rough and dangerous Harris Hill grade and join the Hunter Mountain road. Once in late May, I wanted to try the Hunter Mountain road and the Rangers at Grapevine Station said, "Well, if you make it in that rig, let us know. There was four feet of snow there when we tried it two days ago." The mountains that ring Death Valley are not always arid. But this fork was marked by a famous post. It was called Teakettle Junction, and on the signpost were old coffee pots and battered teakettles which had been hung there in jest. But it is a sad tribute to the demonic spirit so strong in our times, that when I was there in the fall of 1981 some vandals had not only shot the sign full of holes and torn it down, but stolen all the picturesque vessels. I collected the spent shells and brought them back to the ranger, who was full of quiet fury at the news. I went there again six months later, but the sign had not been replaced.

This wickedness is not confined to our country. Once, while walking the Cornish Coast Path, I found that the fine oak guide posts had been wantonly sawed down. It was a particularly evil thing to do, since the trail path runs across desolate moors and close to sheer, six-hundred-foot drops into the ocean. In fog or dusk, a lost hiker might easily lose his life. I sent a contribution to the Coastal Path Society in Cornwall, partly in thanks for making this marvelous walk possible, and partly to replace the vandalized signs. That is a proper text in Deuteronomy, "Cursed be he who removeth his neighbor's landmark."

You can see Racetrack a long way before you reach it, a tan flatness with a jagged black mass of rock at the north end. This is Racetrack, and the black mass is the Grandstand. Racetrack is a rather famous place and its main feature, the travelling rocks, has been seen on the pages of *National Geographic*. Large stones, some weighing several hundred pounds, migrate across the flat playa, and their tracks can clearly be seen in the dried mud. It is conjectured that when the lake bed is slippery with rain and a high wind comes up, the rocks are blown for some distance, occasionally making curves and angles in their courses. While this is the most likely theory, it still remains mere theory, since no man has actually observed them in motion. I have never seen Racetrack without superb clouds against the clean blue, casting great gliding shadows on the cliff of the Cottonwood Mountains and the slopes of Ubehebe Peak. Racetrack doesn't stun or awe; it charms.

At the south end the road leads down into Saline Valley, but the lip of the drop is marked with a sign which bars passenger cars. I have walked down the very steep slope, with several old mines off to the left, and someday I hope to get there early enough in the day to walk down to the Lippincott Lead Mine. The road to that point is fairly good, I have heard, but beyond the mine, I was informed by a gal Ranger, it is extremely hazardous even for the best of rigs. There is a side-camber to the lower road down into Saline, and the tilt is so great that it would be well to take the air out of the tires on the upper side in order to lessen the danger of a tip-over and a perhaps fatal descent into the chasm. It is a trip I would like to take but never will; it's probably too much for Excelsior, and certainly too much for me.

# 8

# Greenwater

Greenwater is a seldom visited valley, and with some reason. It has no striking geological features and the scenery is merely pleasant, not grand. It lies east of the southern end of Death Valley—a long shallow vale with the Greenwater Range on the east and the Black Mountains on the west. The jagged eastern boundary of Death Valley takes in part of it. I include it in this account because it is a fine example of how quickly nature comes in to take over when man leaves, a view which will be questioned by environmentalists, who, I think, tend to underestimate the recuperative power of nature.

On a bright winter's morning when the chill was going out of the desert air, I was driving along a seldom-travelled road that runs from Shoshone to Death Valley, my son Jack at my side. It is a thirty-mile stretch up the Greenwater Valley and the first eleven miles are miserable by reason of the number of washes that must be crept across and the rocks that bestrew the unmaintained road. It isn't dangerous; it's just slow, jolty going. Late last November we had lurched up that trail with dark coming down and had not realized that off to our left was the ghost town of Greenwater. Returning home, I had read of the town in an account which said, "There miners rushed to what promoters advertised as the greatest copper camp on earth, but the hopeful, the gullible, and the drifters were left with little to do but nurse their futile dreams . . . not a single one of the 2,500 recorded claims brought in anything worthwhile. But the town, whose population grew to about a thousand, had several saloons, stores, a bank, a post office, two newspapers, and even telephone service. It also had its share of shenanigans and shootouts." Historian

Harold Weight notes that "After the death of Billy Robinson following a prolonged binge . . . the saints, the sinners, and the inbetweens all attended Billy's rites, and Tiger Lil placed five aces in his hand, pressed close to his breast, 'so he'll look natural.'"

Obviously, this was a town worth visiting, and after carefully reading the tenths of miles between trails indicated by the Auto Club map, we drove along a smooth road through the chaparral on the easy slopes of the Black Mountains. But there was nothing but sage in sight. "Where's the town?" asked my son. And I said, "We are in it." At the crossroads was a post, and on it a recent sign saying "Greenwater, 4380," and a number of refreshingly non-obscene graffiti—"Tom and Bill and Ed wasted their time and gas coming to this place," "The night life here is not riotous," and my son added the words, "Greenwater, room for 250,000. Bring your own water." We went up the road to Greenwater Spring, a drop-by-drop trickle from a rusty pipe, and came back to town to make camp for the night. I say town, but there was absolutely nothing standing. All through the brush were strewn the boards, beams, and clapboards of old houses demolished by the rains and winds. There were rusty kerosene cans, and interestingly, many vestiges of old hand-cranked telephone batteries—carbon rods with a little zinc paste left on them.

After clearing the truck and gathering wood against the coming night, I went for a walk. I climbed a knoll and looked out on the empty and beautiful valley. To the east lay the Greenwater Mountains, to the west the Black Mountains that stand over southern Death Valley. Far, far to the north and blued by distance, stood the Last Chance Range, and to the southeast were the snow-crowned summits of the Spring Range in Nevada. Save for a faint yellow tracery of sandy roads through the green chaparral, there was no sign of man's handiwork. The valley was clean, empty, as serene as it was ten thousand years ago. As I sat in the icy wind by the dying campfire that night I was deeply impressed by the almost total disappearance of man's handiwork, and the continuing strength of the tough green growth and the eternal hills. I wrote a sermon about the episode (p. 136) saying that the ghost town of Greenwater was a profound and subtle parable of the human condition apart from God. The brightest of earthly hopes are doomed, and only the hopes grounded in God are eternal. I preached the sermon in many places, including London, and I consider it one of the best I have done in my half-century of homiletic toil.

I mention Greenwater in this essay in part because it alone of all the valleys I have visited was the scene of a specific religious act. I often quietly worship God in the outback, and stand in bareheaded contemplation of creation, but seldom, perhaps because I am so often alone, is there any hint of formal worship on my trips. There is one shining exception.

On Mother's Day, 1982, I took a group to Greenwater; some of the party who had heard me preach about it in London wanted to see if it really is as desolate as I had sermonically described it. It was, they agreed; only utter ruin where once a town had briefly flourished. Saturday night a fierce cold wind roared down on us from the Black Mountains; the trucks rocked and had to be moored head into the gale, like boats in a windswept harbor. Two women of the party felt that Mothers' Day should be celebrated even in this sage-green emptiness. And so with the wind subsiding but still gusting, we had our service. Barbara Wright racked her memory for a hymn verse to serve as a call to worship; Bernice Gamage gave a brief, brokenly-eloquent sermon, and I said the prayer. It was a small congregation, not much over Christ's essential two or three; a service held in a vast house not built by hands, a temple with mountain-range walls, and the pale arching roof of the immense sky. But God was very close.

*Hedgehog Cactus along Racetrack Road*

# 9

# Butte

Butte Valley is small, remote, and lovely. It has a haunting quality about it, perhaps because it is relatively lush. Three fine springs—Anvil, Greater View, and Willow—water it, and it once was the feeding grounds for burros in such numbers as I have never seen elsewhere. In two-wheel drive it can be approached only from the east. It lies between the southern ends of Death Valley and Panamint Valley, and the road is formidable on the last two miles coming west, of which passage I shall later speak. To get to it you go out of Baker, California, up the route towards Shoshone and turn off the pavement at Wade's Exit. This road follows the course of the northward-flowing Amargosa River which empties into Death Valley. It is usually dry, but it can be sticky, and I tell an incident of that stickiness.

    I once led a small safari up the Amargosa River road towards Butte Valley. While we were still on hard surface, we saw ahead of us a heavy rainstorm. The clouds were purple, and the gray veils of rain were thick. We were in sunshine, but there was an authentic cloudburst ahead, and we might be running into a flash flood. We went through a heavy shower, but when we left the pavement the sky was clear. We had no problem until we came to the Owl Hole Spring turn-off. Straight ahead lay the road to the southern end of Death Valley; it was grimly marked. "Bad Road," "Four Wheel Drive Only," "Not Patrolled Daily," "Difficult Crossing Twelve Miles Ahead." But what was worse, standing water lay across the road; the cloudburst had been heavy here. If alone, I would have turned back, but the party was eager to go on, so we started up the road, poor at best, and now holding a dismal possibility of getting mired.

We slipped and slithered along, with me in the lead. I was worried about a little 1800cc Courier crewed by twin sisters, but every time I stopped beyond a bad place the Courier was close behind. I was not concerned about the big, three-quarter-ton camper driven by Don Helsel; its 454 cid engine and huge back tires were our insurance, for should a lesser rig get stuck, the powerful truck could haul it out.

I was amazed at the extent of the flash flood. I thought it would be confined to a few washes, but for several miles the water had poured down the entire mountain side, and the road was a long bog. I worried about getting across the Amargosa River. I had travelled this route a number of times, but always in dry or cold weather. When we came to the river I stopped in dismay. It was not too wide, a hundred yards at the most, and not too deep, perhaps a foot of water in the deepest part. But what the bottom might be like, I did not know. The others pulled up behind me, and I waded the muddy stream. There was an exceedingly slippery mud, but under that the bottom seemed firm and good. I still hesitated; I often go alone to the outback and I have developed a caution which spills over into sheer timidity at times. "Go on, Doc," said Don. "You can make it."

I wasn't at all sure, but with my companion in the cab beside me, we hit the water with a run. Some delicacy is needed here. If you go too slow, you run the risk of losing momentum and getting bogged down. If you hit it too fast, you are in danger of having the resultant splash drown your motor. But Excelsior made it to the other shore, and the Courier, plugging along in his track, also triumphed. The big camper started across, made the first channel, then slowed and stopped on a middle bar, genuinely stuck. Don, a veteran, was not dismayed. He put us all to work bringing rocks which he put under the jacked-up rear wheel. He also had us working to make a hard slope in front of all four wheels, and he was ready for the rush for solid ground. He stuck again, despite our pushing, and he backed off. One of the pushing group, caught off balance by the truck's retreat, fell into the sticky mud and lay helpless. A camera bug in the party whipped out her little instrument and heartlessly besought him not to get up until she had captured his plight for later mockery. He was understandably cold to this appeal and the color shot shows him on his knees, hands misshapen with clay, struggling to his feet. We finally got the big camper across.

We decided to stay there for the night, and we had a splendid cocktail time (an hour is too small a span) while a strong hot wind blew. I walked up to see the shape of the road to come, and found it fair, but not too encouraging. We were very near sea level and the road was dropping; there might be settled water and mire ahead. In the morning the river was much lower; the drying night wind had done its work. So we started off toward hard surface to the north, another twelve miles away. The road worsened as we went, and suddenly, seeing nothing but a long narrow pond ahead where the road should have been, on impulse I yanked the steering wheel hard left and shot out onto the firm ground of the roadside. The Courier followed, but the big camper, following closely, braked a bit, and was dismally stuck.

There was more shovelling in the ankle-deep, incredibly tenacious clay, and the ridge at roadside was flattened. I hitched up Excelsior to the truck, and with both engines roaring, and my all-terrain tires grabbing, we pulled the few feet to hard ground. I had gone off just at the right time. Had I continued a hundred yards further, we would have all been hopelessly stuck and had to wait for days until the ground dried out. We got turned around, recrossed the river, easier now, and went back to the pavement to finish the trip. We were eleven miles short of our goal in Death Valley when we turned back. We travelled over a hundred miles to get to that point by good road.

Incidentally, the big camper should not be faulted for being stuck. It was carrying too large a load, and on the next trip the camper body was left behind and the bare truck did the travelling. It is an axiom among back country drivers that "they can all get stuck." There is no machine which can conquer any road. I remember once, travelling the beach of the Sea of Cortez in Baja California, when the rig I was in, a Ford Bronco —4WD, big tires, a seasoned driver—got caught in a pebbly trench at water's edge with the tide coming in. When the other trucks in the party were hitched on with long wire cables, it took good drivers and three big motors in low, low gear to get that truck out of trouble. For this reason experienced back country drivers prefer to go in pairs or trios rather than alone. Later on that same trip we came to a pass described as "hazardous, even for 4WDs." It had been recently washed out by a flash flood, and we looked at it askance; but since we didn't have gas enough to go back, we pressed on. It took forty-five minutes to get the first vehicle, a big wide V8 Jeep, through the first fifteen feet of a gorge so narrow that there was only room for two of my fingers on one side of the tonneau and my thumb on the other. We entered that two-mile defile at six in the evening; we came to the pass at midnight; our speed was a third of a mile an hour. I later wrote a sermon about this episode (p. 95). I call it "You Have to Go in Convoy" and discuss the inescapable human need for mutual help, not only in the back country, but on all of life's trails.

I had been attracted to Butte Valley by Ed Sanders' book, *The Family,* which tells of the Manson Family's murders and their entrapment in the Myers Ranch which lay just below Mengel Pass. We were fascinated by the notion of following Charlie and his slaves through this bad stretch of trail. When Jack and I first essayed it, we came up the mine road to Warms Springs rather easily, but when we turned left for the long climb into the higher valley we would never have known where the road was had it not been for a tiny sign. The road itself was almost indiscernable. We were overtaken by night, and the hollows and ruts and great stones looked even worse in the headlights than they actually were, which was bad enough. We pulled off finally and waited till daylight for the rest of the passage.

For a long time we climbed and then dropped. Finally the formation that gives the place its name came into view. The butte is a striking pyramid of rock, shaped somewhat like Gibraltar, and it rises, gorgeous with great black and white stripes, out of a pale green valley. We stopped at Anvil Springs where stands a fine stone house with a superb view. There is a small, constantly flowing spring in front of it, with a single brave big cottonwood. The mud around the spring is stippled with beast tracks, mostly burros, and small birds dive and twitter in the air. The house was built in 1880 by someone whose name is not remembered.

A quarter of a mile away is another house with a smaller spring. Perhaps to compensate for less water, this spring is known as Greater View. From that fine vantage point you can look toward a patch of greener green nested at the base of Needle Peak. This is Willow Spring, and I have read that for disciplinary reasons Charlie Manson would make his girls (those daughters of affluent Westchester and like suburbs) walk barefooted at night to bring water over the long rough miles back to the ranch, although there was good water at the ranch and nearby Sourdough Spring. From Willow Spring a poor road leads into the hills.

Beyond Greater View the trail leads to Mengel Pass before descending into Panamint Valley. At the summit, fifty feet outside the border of Death Valley Monument, there is a cairn of stones, bound with an iron hoop, memorializing the death in 1944 of Carl Mengel, the one-legged prospector who used the pass. Formerly the cairn was topped by a shaft of wood; on the shaft was one of Carl's battered and weather-dried boots. Some conscienceless souvenir collector has recently stolen both stick and shoe.

The Goler Wash jeep trail is very steep and stony, and when, eight years ago, my son and I first tackled it, we did so with some trepidation; our little Datsun was not exactly the rig for such a passage. A ranger whom we consulted doubted if we could make it, but he did not forbid us passage. One veteran in a jeep said, "You can make it all right, but you'll have to build road." At first it wasn't too bad, and when we got to the proper turn-off we went to look at the Myers Ranch. It was an eerie place; the lingering scent of depravity tainted the air. We could not find the green school bus which Charles Manson managed to drive in from Shoshone, and where it has gone is a mystery. But we did find the abandoned house and the machine gun placements where Charlie expected to hold off the hordes of blacks who would ravish California when "Helter Skelter" (his code name for Armageddon) came.

We went to the ranch where Charlie and his family holed up after the Tate-La Bianca murders. In the yard was a gruesome dumb show, by which Charlie had terrified a mutinous follower—a low gravestone, with a cap in front of it and, some six feet away, a pair of boots, half-buried, toes up. It is probable that had it not been for a bit of foolish deviltry the family might have stayed safely hidden in this desolate refuge, but they elected, out of pure cussedness, to burn up a skip-loader which the Park Service had just purchased out of scanty funds. This was the last straw. The Rangers, the Highway Patrolmen, and the lawmen of Inyo County made a concerted raid on the ranch. It was an easy capture, for if the ranch was isolated, it was also easy to block off, since there was but one trail. I remember the description of the arrest. All the other people were taken, but Charlie was not to be found. At last an officer lighted a bit of candle and explored the bathroom. He opened a closet underneath the sink and there was the tiny multiple murderer. He surrendered with no struggle. As we looked about I saw on the table the stub of the candle, or at least, it might well have been the very one that lighted the capture of the man whom *Time* recently called "the dark star of the inmate nation." I picked up the stub for a souvenir and carried it in my car for a time. A hot day reduced it to a pool of wax at the bottom of my glove compartment.

Here I feel an urge to insert a lurid tale which does not properly belong in a narrative of the Valleys, but it has pertinence. On a blazingly hot August day in 1968, I was sitting in the only shade I could find, a couple of feet of shelter from the sun cast by the deserted jailhouse in the ghost town of Garlock. As I sat there with sandwich and can of ginger ale, a black sedan came up from the south, slowed as it passed me, stopped after a couple of hundred yards, and came back. It passed me scarcely thirty feet away, for the jail doorstep touched the hard surface, and I saw that the car was driven by a little man with a great black beard, and his comrades were evil-appearing wretches. They went on toward Mojave, then stopped and started up again. My antenna were vibrating rapidly. I went to the back of my car, opened the trunk, and as they paused, ostentatiously pumped six magnum .22s into my Ruger. Then I sat down by the door step; at my right hand were my cocked gun, sandwich, and drink.

Sure enough, a few hundred yards north they turned and started back. I was curiously detached and calm. I thought (and the idiom was not common to me), "If you get your jollies beating up old men, don't try me. I won't be easy." The black car slowed to a crawl opposite me; the bearded driver glared at me, and no word passed between us. I was quietly resolved to kill the driver instantly if he opened the door. I had a single action gun; I had to pull back the hammer for each discharge, and I could not afford the moral luxury of a warning shot. I figured I could also get the second man out—it was a four-door sedan— and might get the third one; I felt that in hand-to-hand battle I could handle the fourth man. The car halted; perhaps ten feet separated us. We locked eyes in voiceless confrontation.

Then the driver stepped on it, laid down rubber, and disappeared to the south. As I munched and drank, I wondered why my hackles had risen so fast, why the fetor of peril hung in the air. Then I suddenly realized. We were near Goler Heights (a long way from Goler Wash but named after the same prospector). A few weeks before I had been told by the recluse who was watchman for the Holland Mine in Iron Canyon, that the Manson gang, not then of such ill-fame as was later to be theirs, had a hang-out in a hollow near Garlock. Not long after that I read in the *Los Angeles Times* that the nude, ravished body of a girl had been found not far from that spot. The coroner estimated that she had been dead about ten days. The pack had found easier prey than an armed old man.

I have perhaps bored my friends to whom I have told this tale with my repetitious analysis of my post-episodic moral scruples. As far as I could tell the first man was unarmed, but had he opened the door and moved towards me, I would have killed him without compunction. I can understand killing in hot blood, in the rage of combat. But as I think back I am appalled at my lack of emotion. I was not excited; I was not even frightened. It was a wordless game with mortal stakes; someone must die. It wasn't going to be me if I could help it. My inner problem was, and is, that I was calmly entertaining thoughts that should be alien to a minister of the Gospel. I did not know my dark side was that dark. Of course, it can be argued that I had a right to defend myself; but it is my utter lack of emotion that still troubles me.

A further thought. If the man was in fact Charles Manson (and I am 99 and 44/100 per cent sure that it was) how would his death at that moment have altered the history of crime? I am hazy at this point, but I am pretty sure that this event took place before the perpetration of the Family's vilest crime, the Tate-La Bianca killings. If the little bearded man had been Manson, and if he had opened the door, would Sharon Tate still be alive and the baby cruelly murdered in her womb have become a vital teen-ager? Two 'ifs' are pretty conjectural, but the thought sometimes occurs to me as I drive by Garlock jail and remember.

We left the ranch and headed for Panamint Valley. To this point the warning sign (now gone) at the eastern entrance of the trail—"This is a dangerous road. No services for 57 miles."—seemed a bit grim. But we found the reason in the last two miles, for the road led over the infamous Seven Dry Falls. The owner of the Myers Ranch had once maintained the road, but after the heavy rains of the winter of 1947 the road was left unmaintained, and it is necessary literally to drive over seven small falls. It is rugged going—one man out front hand-signalling "Come ahead about six inches," or "two or three inches to your right," while the man at the wheel (Jack in this case) edges the machine over ridges and rocks unfit for traversing in anything except a short wheelbase, high-clearance 4WD.

We were lucky that time, escaping with only dents in the rear corners and badly wrenched alignment, and once out we swore we would never try it again. But the next time we had a 4WD escort, and it was a long way back to Furnance Creek and gas. A skilled driver with us offered to guide Jack down, but he was less skilled than I at this point, for the truck got badly hung up, and it took some doing to free it. Just as we came out into the open alluvial fan of the canyon, we found that the rocks had removed the slave cylinder of the clutch; we could only run in high. After a mile of stony descent it was smooth and level till Ballarat, where we hoped to get help. But the woman who had opened a little store had given up and gone. If we could get to Trona, 28 miles further on, we were safe, but it is a steep climb out of Panamint, and the truck could not possibly make it in high gear. At the critical point in the grade, with motor and wheels in sync, Jack made a perfect clutchless shift down into third. The Sergeant, stout fella, given remedial treatment in Trona, responded nobly and healed himself as we went, so that when we reached Los Angeles, the clutch worked perfectly.

Just before Christmas 1982, Jack and I drove up to the western mouth of Goler Wash. Making the pleasurable discovery that a mining company had graded the dry falls so that they were rather easily ascended, we drove up to the Barker Ranch. An astonishing and excellent transformation had taken place. Plastic hoses dripped water about the bases of the fig trees, the pomegranates had ripened and the birds had feasted on them. The door was unlocked and inside all had been swept and garnished and painted. The washroom where Charlie had cowered was clean, and on the wall was a sign asking all who entered to treat the place with care. But the utterly unexpected sight was the south wall of the main room. The white mantelpiece held a jovial Santa, "a stocking was hung by the chimney with care," and in the center was a tall Christ candle. Some Forest Rangers or imaginative back country drivers had changed what was once a habitation of foul creatures, an apartment in the suburbs of hell, into a place where Christ's coming was remembered. It was a totally unexpected and refreshing statement of the dual nature of man, and I wrote a sermon about it. Unfortunately, in the spring of 1982, when I tried to bring a safari up to see this good sight, we found that the heavy winter rains had washed away the grading and left the road much as it had been—strictly 4WD country. I took a shot at it and was immediately and ignobly stuck on the first fall, slippery with running water. We were forced to alter our itinerary drastically.

The persistent lure of Butte Valley brought a small group of us back for a two-night stay in the spring of 1983. We found that Anvil Spring house had been repaired by a group of men from a service station in Whittier; the door was unlocked and visitors were asked to leave the place "better than you found it." With delight we made camp and leisurely savored the valley. We found a third house, Russell's Camp, tucked away in a canyon beyond Greater View. A pleasant young man who was staying there briefly said that none of these houses—Anvil, Greater View, and Russell's Camp—had any legitimate ownership. The Bureau of Land Management had taken them in 1975, and they now live in sufferance. Only the rulings of James Watt, he said, who felt that mining claims should be honored, kept them from being demolished.

Personally I cannot understand the thinking of the environmentalists who would raze these old structures, which blend marvelously with the landscape and provide shelter for the appreciative back country travellers who occasionally occupy them. A number of years ago I was much impressed by Robinson Jeffers' book on the Big Sur area, *Not Man Apart*, in which he said that man must not consider himself remote from nature, alien from it, but part of it. And were not the ranchers and miners who worked this valley, and lived in it, and loved it, a part of the environment? These camps are not blots on the desert; they belong there. A bit of the fascination of the desert is the fact that man lives in it, passes through it, comes to love it. I find myself resenting the dogmatic elitism of environmentalist groups which deny to seekers after solitude and beauty the right to go to places where these groceries of the soul may be had.

It is hard to analyze the compelling charm of Butte Valley. Perhaps it lies in the tortured angularity of the zebra-striped butte itself; perhaps in the greenness of the valley veined with the crooked golden thread of its north-running road and the brown and black walls of the sheltering mountains that encircle it. Or it might be the burro families that graze and play and fight and sidle up to the spring for their evening drink; it might lie in the solitary cottonwood that towers over the spring, a gathering place for all manner of darting birds; perhaps it is the remoteness and solitude of the place, an increment from the barrier of the nine miles of villainous rocky road that leads into it; possibly the lingering presence of Carl Mengel casts a benign spell. It's hard to say. At all events, we had already half-decided to return when a herd of four mule deer, two does, two fawns, came in from the north and passed by less than fifty yards from our window, big-eared, alert for the sight or sound of the truculent and cruel-hoofed burros who claim the spring as possession. Back and forth the lovely creatures drifted, ever edging toward the water, and finally, thirst quenched, passed from our sight in an adagio ballet of grace and beauty. That rare and splendid viewing was the climax of our feast of seeing, and it settled the issue; we decided to go back for an even longer stay.

We did; in the spring of 1984 I took a group in for a four-day stay. The safari had two purposes. The main one was to satisfy our hunger for Butte Valley, for with but one exception every person I have taken in there wants to stay longer. The other was a desire to explore the valley, and particularly Redlands Canyon, through which, legend has it, the Bennett-Arcane party went on its escape from death at the famous Long Camp. Seven years earlier, on our second trip in, Brad Hagie had gone part way down the canyon on his Honda trail bike, but had turned back before reaching the end. He had been told at Ballarat that the trail ended in a sheer twenty-foot cliff, which had required the pioneers to dismantle their wagons and rope them down over the cliff to the bottom, where they were reassembled. Previously two of us had driven down in Excelsior as far as we dared, and walked further without reaching the cliff. We wanted to try it again, to see if we could round the last of the canyon's beckoning bends and view the rarely-visited drop that troubled the pioneers a century-and-a-half ago.

We assembled at my house early on a Monday morning, five trucks and nine people, and sailed the freeways and hard surface through Barstow, Baker, and Shoshone; we skipped the Amargosa road this time. I had prepared the newcomers for a gruelling grind into the Valley after leaving Warm Springs, but we discovered that the road in had been graded smooth; I named it "Butte Valley Boulevard." We greeted this with mingled feelings. The passage in was now easy, which took some of the adventure out of the trip and also made the Valley perhaps too easily accessible. And we knew the road had been smoothed so that the Park Rangers, in their program of getting rid of the Death Valley burro population, could transport trapped burros out for adoption or to the dog food factories. We saw one sad lone burro near Warm Springs, which was an ill omen. It wasn't all that bad, however; we reckon the valley has a present population of forty. But gone are the herds totalling over three hundred which we had seen before.

It was 102°F at the south end of the Westside Road in Death Valley, and we worried about the heat. It was an unnecessary anxiety. The first night a howling cold front moved in; the wind roared down the canyon, and the two women in the party who slept out had to rope their beds down. The temperature the next morning was 40°F, and thermals felt good. It made for a pleasant stay, unseasonably cool and delightful.

On the first morning we found that the yarn about the 20 foot drop in Redlands Canyon was a myth. In his van Brad had brought a 500cc, one-lunged Kawasaki, with elephantine torque, and he went down the canyon ahead of us. We left our trucks at Bathroom Junction (as far as we dared drive) and followed him down on foot. My trick left knee, a souvenir of my old basketball wars, gave out in the rough rubble, and I couldn't go as far as the women did. Returning, Brad met them part way and said that the goal wasn't worth it; there was no dramatic sheer drop, only a jumble of big rocks which blocked the view of Panamint Valley. So much for local information.

The four days made an idyllic time of discovery. We had the valley to ourselves with the exception of a bunch of middle-aged motorcyclists (Not "Hell's Angels" types) who appeared at Anvil Spring, idiotically wondering if there was a gas station around the corner. Fortunately, they had enough gas between them to cover the 69 miles back to Furnace Creek, the nearest fuel supply. Their foolishness in visiting the far outback without abundant reserves of gas indicates why the desert claims a lethal toll of death by thirst every summer.

Brad found what local lore says are two outlaw caves, hidden in a tumble of huge rocks and commanding a view of the whole valley, in case a posse should be approaching. The main cave roofed by an enormous stone slab had a crude chimney and was loosely chinked with rocks against the wind and rain. The number of rusty tin cans, including the rare three-gallon kerosene containers common some sixty or seventy years ago, gives credence to the story that this was a California Hole-in-the-Wall rendezvous, or at least a place of primitive residence. I doubt if the hippie invasion of the Sixties found this spot.

*Hole in the Wall—Mojave*

With difficulty we went up a gulch unnamed on the map but locally known as Wood Canyon, and at trail's end we found a marvelously neat little aluminum cabin, doubtless owned by a modern claim-holder. The road was steep and in one place dangerously sandy; but Don Helsel twisted Excelsior's tail, and with the tach revving high, the truck went bounding up the grade, big tires grabbing and limited slip differential hard at work. Marian Mathews and Bernice Gamage, precariously perched on the big Kawasaki, were ferried to road's end. Looking down from above the camp we saw a cluster of color—the big green cedar over the shining silver cabin with Excelsior's orange hood sticking out of the shade; two tanks, one rusty brown and the other painted white; a great gray rock on warm red dirt; with the treeless black face of Manley peak in the background—all under the intense canyon-blue sky. There was an engineering mystery above the cabin: two huge rocks, linked by a thick steel cable, serving no discernable purpose.

We walked part way up Needle Peak to look at its white scars from close range. David Wright was the top walker; he never used his truck during the whole stay; his L. L. Bean walking staff was his one aid to travel. One bad fact: while 1983 saw the record rain in Death Valley, 4.54 inches, 1984 was a record dry year, with no precipitation at all by mid-May. Butte Valley was a barren brown, not its customary pale green, a hard summer for the beasts of that place.

We stayed at Russell's Camp, a building begun in 1911 and added to in 1933, so inscriptions pencilled on the kitchen wall told us. Russell and Huhn, two gold seekers, had come into Butte Valley in the early 1920s with a three months' truckload of supplies. After hot and weary work they found a marvelously rich gold lode, only to lose it when torrential rains washed out their markers. They never could find it again. "There's gold in them thar hills." The camp is a sprawling set of locust-shaded, tin-roofed wooden structures, with much long-unused heavy mining gear lying about, and a white, weathered burro's skull stuck on the topmost branch of the tree at the entrance. The kitchen had an incredible rarity—running water in the sink, piped down from the spring higher on the hill. This greatly eased the chores of meal-getting and pan-washing. The meals, prepared on a propane stove, were ample and tasty.

Quickly the days fell into a pattern; a major exploration in the morning, light lunch, a nap, minor scouting about in the afternoon, and then long pleasant cocktail times, waiting for moonrise. They were truly happy hours with stories and songs and watching the evening shadows creep across the Valley and climb the far hills. On a previous trip Bernice Gamage had taken a picture of the moon rising over the eastern ridges—a brooding purple-toned shot that somehow captured the beauty and loneliness of the desert. She could not repeat it. True, the full moon did come up—huge, golden, cloud-clean over the sharp dark mountain—but somehow this time the road and the lower ridges were cancelled in a hard chiaroscuro. Before the late moon rose on succeeding evenings, the stars were bright and many, and sharp-eyed Brad, an ex-fighter pilot, showed us tumbling satellites turning like silver fish in the perpetual sunlight of space. The days and nights went by as in dream-time; there was no rigid prosaic clock-time. We came; almost at once, it seemed, we had to leave. But the days and nights were gems of back country experience—a lonesome valley, a company of compatible people, no tension or surly silence; dependable, well-found trucks; no phones, no newspapers—a time so flawless that I am superstitiously hesitant to try it again, lest repetition bring bickering, accident, bad weather, or some other cause for regret. It was a peaceful time in a peaceful valley.

# 10

# Beasts, Birds, Flowers, and Rocks

This should be a long informative section, but it won't be, because I'm not sharp of eye nor keen of ear. It is my guess that these dullnesses have caused me to miss much. I cite one instance. One night I was walking with two sisters up the wash that leads northward out of Mesquite Springs, and one of them said, "Dr. B., there's a rattlesnake by your feet." And sure enough the flashlight revealed a sidewinder, neither seen nor heard by me, sounding off his warning not far from my ankles. I killed him with my stick and afterwards felt remorse, since I was invading his range. It could be argued that the buzz of a sidewinder isn't loud, and the girls were keen-eared professional violinists, but even so I can't claim high marks for hearing and seeing. Further, I am lamentably ignorant in technical matters. Thoreau is almost glib the way he gives out with the Latin name of every plant or creature he saw around Walden Pond, along the Concord and Merrimack, as well as on Cape Cod and in the Maine woods. I know virtually nothing about the flora, fauna, and stones of the desert, and I shall simply narrate what I have encountered.

### The Beasts

I speak of beasts first. I have told of burros and Butte Valley deer and shall say no more about them. Once, a quarter of a century ago in the foothills of the San Gabriels overlooking Antelope Valley, I saw a lordly stag with his harem of two does. On the old, endlessly curving Ridge Route, a bright-eyed, black-and-white masked badger once looked at me and leisurely went his way. Twice red foxes have whirled across my path; once a surprised wildcat glared and disappeared. Coyotes, those wise and fierce predators, are common. Coming out of my mobile home park I have twice almost bumped into one as I walked in the shadows and he was in the bright street light. I have never seen the scarce big horn sheep that haunt the high places of the Panamints. Once, as I sat in the dusk, drowsy from a long day and two stiff Scotches, I saw what I thought was an incredibly-swift horned toad scuttle over my shoe. But it was a kangaroo rat, soon joined by another seeker after cracker crumbs. A strange and wonderful ballet-battle began. Kangaroo rats have been timed to move at 17.4 feet a second, and by reason of their long tails they can shift directions in mid-flight of their prodigious leaps. One fled, beaten, and the other nibbled at my feet. They are crepuscular creatures, and when the bright full moon made daylight of the campsite he went away and I did not see him again.

I remember with singular pleasure the case of a mountain lion that escaped from a movie set in the El Pasos, but remained so tame that she leaped into a pickup truck owned by a man who was then the caretaker of the Holland Mine, and waited expectantly for a ride back up Iron Canyon. He worried lest her tameness get her shot by a hunter. He met me one day as I was starting up toward Black Mountain Wash, and on hearing that I was going by Mine #6 told me that she was staying there and to watch out for her, for she now had a kitten. I thanked him for letting me know for I was carrying my big Smith and Wesson .45 revolver, handloaded for bear, and it would have been a shame to shoot at her if she was trying to defend her baby. So all the way past Mine #6 I kept calling loudly, "It's only me, Mrs. Mountain Lion. I won't hurt your kitten." If she were there, this lunatic hooting would have sent her far away. So I went through the narrows of Black Mountain Wash, with its walls of many colored rock —red, black, orange, sand—until I came to a spring. Rusty pipes indicated that it had once given drink to miners of yesterday. I went up the wash a bit further and found a waterhole. It is not marked on any map that I know of, but I have named it Cottonwood Spring because of the little grove that it waters. There was only a shallow pool by the trees, but clear on the damp clay beside it were two sets of paw-marks, one huge and circular, the other of like shape, but a third of the size. The solitary mother had brought her baby there for a drink.

My favorite adventure with beasts did not take place in the desert, but in Devil's Punch Bowl, overlooking Antelope Valley. As I sat eating my lunch after a hike one winter's noon, I looked across one of the immaculately clean tables of the park, and astonishingly saw, not twenty feet away, a gray fox, one diminutive forepaw lifted and curled, looking at me with apprehension but not fear. I was eating fried chicken, and knowing that any motion on my part might mean his disappearance, I ventured to throw a piece of the skin near him. I could hardly say that he moved, so fast was his reaction, but instantly he was in another place. Yet the fragrance of the food made his nose wrinkle, and he edged forward. A swoop, and the tidbit was gone. I tossed another piece, nearer this time, and the process was repeated. Closer and closer I lured him, until he was only six or eight feet away from the other side of the table. I tried to get him to take food from the far-side seat, but this was a little too much for him. I had run out of skin and was giving him my lunch, but Colonel Sanders is open all the time, and wild foxes come for feeding only once in a lifetime. I got him around to my side of the table with well-placed lure, and I could examine him at leisure.

He was outrageously beautiful. Small, with an immense gray brush, a touch of red on his chops, great alert eyes, a long delicate muzzle that opened to show fine white needle-sharp teeth. His paws were tiny, catlike. He was obviously young, inexperienced, or he would not have come so near man. By now I was reduced to bread and butter, and I got him within two or three feet of me. But he would not take a piece from the toe of my boot. He withdrew a few feet and began to groom himself; I lamented the lack of a camera. He was framed in manzanita bushes, and beyond him I could see the distant South Fork trail saddle. He yawned as if bored. Then I broke out a few chocolate-covered graham crackers. Instantly an electric shock went through him. His eyes became enormous; his nostrils fairly vibrated; his whiskers angled up; his body quivered; he seemed to dance while standing still. Now as we know, even to our dull noses, dark chocolate is a strong pungent aroma. The sensitive nostrils of a fox, which can catch faint smells coming on the breeze from hundreds of yards away, could hardly take the terrific voltage of odor from rich, overwhelmingly potent chocolate from a few feet away. He was instantly drunk. He went mad. There was no hesitation in the way he pounced on the first bit of cookie on the ground a few feet from me. Then I put a piece of chocolate cracker on my toe. What bread and butter could not do, the desire evoked by the smell and taste of chocolate did. He ran a risk because of that intoxicating smell and taste. He lost all his prudence, his fear of man. His muzzle came within inches; he looked at me wide-eyed; a swoop and the cookie was gone from my boot.

What happened next was not exactly prudent on my part. I took a little piece of cookie and held it out to him. This will seem a tall tale to those who know the shyness of foxes, but he ate it out of my hand. I had no more crackers, but on the forefinger of my left hand there was a smeared chocolate residue. I held out the finger toward him, for him to lap. He came near, looked at me with his excited eyes, and with a sort of gentle bite and quick tongue movement, cleaned my finger. Now here we both ran a risk. He had to overcome his fear of man, the great enemy; and unknown to him, a few inches from my right hand was a .22 magnum derringer (which I had no thought of using, incidentally). That was his risk. Mine was that I was taking a chance of experiencing rabies shots, or becoming known as Nine-Fingered Butman. But he wanted more of the ravishing sweet, and I wanted to say that a wild fox had lapped my finger. We both ran risks; we both got rewards. He had a taste few if any foxes have had, and I had a rare experience, and one which I am not likely to repeat.

It is written, "Now the serpent was more subtle than any beast of the field," which text makes a good transition from mammals to reptiles. Snakes are not too often seen in the true desert, probably because of the heat. Snakes and lizards are "cold blooded," which means that they do not have a built-in thermostat; their internal temperature is that of the surrounding air. Dr. Raymond B. Cowles in his *Desert Journal* speaks with a wide knowledge of those "living thermometers—desert reptiles." When the ambient air hits 120°F in summer, a rattler trapped in the direct rays of the sun will become "hot blooded" and die. The lively little lizards of several sorts do scuttle briskly over rocks in the sun, but snakes stay in the shade or glide about at twilight or dawn, seeking food. The alarm clock rattle of *crotalus durnissus* is an unmistakable noise. I once saw a woman walking ahead of me leap high and sideways, crying "Rattlesnake!" I came near to see a thick-bodied black timber rattler coiled in the grass by the side of the road. She had never heard a rattlesnake before, but she instinctively knew what the metallic clatter meant.

Genesis gives us one explanation of the instinctive enmity between man and the serpent.

> And the Lord said to the snake, You will be punished for this ... I will make you and the woman hate each other; her offspring and yours will always be enemies. Her offspring will crush your head, and you will bite his heels.
> 
> (*Good News Bible*, Gen. 3:14, 15)

I have a powerful ambivalence toward snakes. I am afraid of them and am more at ease sleeping in my truck than on the ground. I once saw one of the thick black timber rattlers that are common in the San Gabriel Mountains near my home. He was coiled in the shadow of a rock in the dry creek bed. Had I been walking the other way and so not able to see him, I might well have had his fangs in my ankle as I stepped off the rock;

for years sharp memory kept him coiled behind that rock; I always walked around it. I strictly observe the advice given me when I first went to the back country: climbing, I never reach up and put my hand where I can't see. Walking, I keep to the open places, away from the mesquite shade. I avoid places where I have previously seen rattlers. My wife, who scorned the possibility of snake bite, was brought to a change of mind by two happenings. Once, getting out of the car, she actually stepped on a sleeping snake and only the somnolence of the drowsy creature let her escape unbitten. Another time she stirred up a "Mojave Green," a particularly dangerous reptile, whose venom, I have heard, attacks both the blood and the nervous system. The ancient enmity is in my blood.

Yet I also know a strong admiration for snakes. Agur, the son of Jaketh, was right when he listed among the four things too wonderful for him, "the way of a serpent upon a rock." How graceful is the going of a snake!—the coiling and reaching, no discernable play of muscles as in the walk of a cat, a silent rippling progress. Even the little horned sidewinder, leaving his strange loopings on the sand, has his own odd charm. One day on a trail near Iron Canyon, I came across a trio of sunning king snakes. They are beautiful, nonvenomous creatures, having the same red, yellow, and black markings that the smaller and deadly coral snake has, but with a different order of banding. I did not want to shoot at them, but I did want to get by, so I tossed a pebble at them. Their speed astonished me; instantly they were brilliant flames in the brush, racing out of harm's way.

For long I killed rattlers on sight, not only because they scared me, but because they posed a threat to the next passerby. But now I leave them alone because they are not aggressive and will get away if they can. The rattlesnake is a gentleman; he does not misuse his killing power by striking in swift deadly silence; he sounds a loud tocsin. I became striken in conscience over this matter when I shot at a rattler who could have fanged me on a narrow trail between thick brush and steep drop off. He sounded his warning. I shot at him coiled, and perhaps hit him; I fired again as he fled. Afterward I was bothered by my desire to kill a fleeing foe who had warned me of his presence. I do not shoot at him now, nor run over him if he crosses the path of my truck. If I stop, wait, make no move at him, in due time he will uncoil and glide away with dignity.

Mankind in general has a blend of fear and respect for the snake; he is a complex symbol of wisdom and healing. In some cultures the snake is worshipped. The nearest we have to that in this country are those fundamentalist cults who consider it a matter of faith to prove Christ's words that true believers may take up serpents with impunity. Be it remembered that Paul, shipwrecked on the isle of Malta, shook off the deadly viper that fastened on his hand and suffered no harm, to the wonder of the natives who considered that his immunity was that of a god. In the deeply textured story of the Fall, the serpent is wiser than man, and with his crafty talk lures Eve to disobedience and the loss of innocence. Jesus told his disciples to be not only as harmless as doves, but wise as serpents. For me the snake is no simple creature. He is beauty and poison, grace and death; he betokens wisdom, which can increase sorrow as well as heal. He is Lucifer, the morning star who fell from heaven and became God's enemy, "that old serpent, Satan." But since he does not seek me out to do me harm, when by chance I now meet him in the wilderness, he is safe from my bullet which is quicker than his fangs and can strike from a greater distance.

The concept of snake as healer is complex. The caduceus—the winged staff with twined serpents—did not originally symbolize benevolent healing, nor was its wisdom white, for it was carried by Hermes, the Greek god of commerce, invention, and cunning. It has a better meaning as a doctor's emblem, for in this usage it goes back to the early healer, Hippocrates, and the god Asclepius. I end this treatment of snakes on a theological note, a strange riddle in Judeo-Christian doctrine. One of the woes Israel encountered in the desert was an infestation of venomous snakes. The perplexing tale is told in Numbers 21:6-9:

> And the Lord sent fiery serpents among the people, and they bit the people; and much people of Israel died.
> 
> Therefore the people came to Moses, and said, We have sinned, for we have spoken against the Lord, and against thee; pray unto the Lord, that he take away the serpents from us. And Moses prayed for the people.
> 
> And the Lord said unto Moses, Make thee a fiery serpent, and set it upon a pole: and it shall come to pass, that every one that is bitten, when he looketh upon it, shall live.
> 
> And Moses made a serpent of brass, and put it upon a pole, and it came to pass, that if a serpent had bitten any man, when he beheld the serpent of brass, he lived.

This is an exceedingly strange story. Sir James Fraser, he of *Golden Bough* fame, would have solved the enigma easily. It was a clear case of imitative magic—like relates to like. A live snake killed people, a brass snake could heal them. But the matter is not that simple. Moses was not long down from Sinai where he had received the Ten Commandments, of which the second was "Thou shalt not make unto thee any graven image" and a graven image—a three-dimensional representation of a living creature—a brass snake certainly was. Further, and even more strange, Moses made and lifted up this image at the express command of God, who thus revoked one of his own big laws. The mystery continues; the people were effectively healed by this idolatrous device. The mystery deepens. In the Gospel of John (3:14) Jesus astonishingly likens himself to this heathen idol: "As Moses lifted up the serpent in the wilderness, even so shall the Son of Man be lifted up." To have a brass snake as a symbol of the crucified Christ is indeed enigmatic, particularly as John, who puts the words in Christ's mouth, later spoke of "that old serpent called the Devil and Satan." The deliberate parallel of the brass reptile who healed the bitten Semites in the wilderness of Sinai with Christ on the cross, healing the spiritual sickness of all kinds, is something to think about.

I have a soft spot in my heart for the desert tortoise, and I ache with fury at the way destructive fools with .22 short or long guns have murdered this gentle, helpless, denizen of the desert. A quarter of a century ago there were many of them around Saddleback Butte in Antelope Valley, but they are gone now. Fifteen years ago there was a great concentration of them north of the town of Mojave on a road then called Neuralia Siding. But then I began to find high domed shells with a single bullet hole in them and cobwebs and new growth across the mouths of many of those distinctive, semi-circular entrances to their dens. The desert tortoise can't run on his relatively long legs, but against natural predators he didn't need to; he simply withdrew into his tough shell and waited out the enemy. But his shell isn't bullet-proof, and he was easy prey for the cruel morons who invaded his domain. This area is now a posted tortoise sanctuary, and I hope it is not too late to save him.

## The Birds

The birds of the desert are many, but since I lack the ornithological eye and mind, I can't say much about them from first hand observation. I have read that most of the desert birds are like their kindred in cooler and wetter places. The beasts avoid the heat problem by burrowing into the cool protection of the earth; the birds escape the blistering heat by migration. They come to the wasteland when the flowers are rich and many and consequently the insect food for adults and nestling is abundant. When the heat comes and the flowers fade, they leave. I have often seen the broad-winged Cooper's hawk, frequently in pairs; and once, rounding a corner of a high canyon trail, I flushed an eagle, a golden confusion of big beating wings and tail feathers spread in transparency. Buzzards are common, high up, riding the strong thermals on apparently motionless wings, until their far-ranging nictitating eyes sight the dead creature, far below and a long way off, that shall serve them for food. Big glossy crows are likewise scavengers. But the desert bird I like best is the roadrunner, that ungainly cartoonist's delight, the mascot of many 4WD clubs. He can run at great speed and seldom flies, but once, coming out of Last Chance Canyon in the El Pasos, I surprised a big roadrunner who did not take so much as a single step but flew straight up into a Joshua tree and stared at me with his shining idiot's eye. Roadrunners are the terror of rattlesnakes it is said, and the deadly serpent will flee like a rabbit from the foe with the long spearlike beak that can strike with superior speed. Roadrunners have been seen with sections of snake dangling from their beaks; they digest a few inches and then gulp in another length of nourishment.

## The Flowers

Books upon books have been written and pictured on the blooms of the desert, for they are many and marvelous. R. S. Ferris in her treatise, *The Flowers of Death Valley*, notes that "by actual count there are between 600 and 700 plants" there, while probably "between 900 and 1000 is a more nearly correct figure." This reckoning is hardly to be classified as scientific precision, but it does indicate the incredible plentitude of flowers in the barren wastes. The great controlling fact of desert flora is water, or rather the lack of it. You can tell the relative scarcity of rain in an area by the distance between mesquite or creosote bushes; the less rain, the greater the space between plants. It takes a given quantity of water to support a bush, and there is a constant, slow, silent, savage battle for it. Desert plants have adapted to the harsh environment in many ways; creosote bushes and tamarisk trees send their tap roots far down, perhaps as far as fifty feet, to drink. Succulents store it; wax or a blanket of fine hairs on the leaves keep water from escaping into the hot windy air. But to write well on the mystery and wonder of floral survival is beyond me. I speak only of personally seen and appreciated beauty.

In Antelope Valley, when the winter rains have been abundant, near Fairmount Buttes the ground is incredibly carpeted—acres and acres of orange poppies, closing as the clouds pass over, opening to the smile of the sun. Bright blue lupine and golden desert dandelions offer rich contrast. Flower lovers in droves make pilgrimage from the cities to be gladdened. But in remote places, seen by few, there are resonances of color against the muted tans and grays of the sand and gravel—big patches of sand verbena, fragrant at night, and after a wet winter the slopes behind Tin Mountain on the way to Racetrack will display a magenta glory of beavertails. It is said that the large reddish blooms of the hedgehog cactus turn into a strawberry-flavored fruit. The crooked, spiny branches of the Joshua tree (oddly, this tall, rough tree is of the lily family) have pale yellow pearls for blossoms. The stately yucca, "the candle of the Lord," sends forth a company of white bell-shaped flowers.

Admittedly, the desert flowers, for over-powering expanse of color, cannot match the bugle call of scarlet maples on New England hillsides in the fall—miles, not acres, of chromatic splendor, bold against the sober green of pines and spruces. But the wonder of desert vegetation lies not only in its splendid and brief exuberance, but in the mere fact that it exists at all. There are, of course, desert areas of such malignant salinity—the Devil's Golf Course and the flats west of Bad Water in Death Valley are samples—where nothing, not even the hardy saltbush, can live. But on ground so dry and hard that the Easterner or the Midwesterner, accustomed to lush meadows and black loam, cannot conceive of leaves and flowers springing from it, there flourishes, spring after spring, an unbelievable wealth of evanescent loveliness. I find delight in it.

But my awe is reserved for a quieter wonder—the tiny flowers that defy the cosmic strength of wind, heat, aridity. This awe had an early origin for me. In the spring of 1953, when I was driving out to candidate at Messiah, I stopped to put foot on the desert I had read so much about. It was a lonely place in Nevada somewhere east of Peach Springs on old Route 66, a desolate spot of great grayness stretching away to angular black mountains under a big sky, forbidding to eyes accustomed to Massachusetts distances. Then at my feet I saw a miracle—a diminutive amethyst bloom perhaps a quarter of an inch across—just one, companionless; an infinitesimal organic growth defying the hostile inorganic immensity that besieged it. Brother Lawrence was brought to a mystic's understanding of God by the sight of a barebranched tree, winter-stripped of its leaves. I was brought to a Wordsworthian mystical experience by the life-force incarnated in a minute blossom in the midst of enormous nonlife. I am still taken by the incongruous delicacy of tiny, richly-colored blooms, clustered for companionship in the midst of sterile sand and rocks shiny with desert varnish. They have a quality of eternity; they will be bearing witness to the unconquerability of life and the reality of beauty when Los Angeles is a waste place under the moon.

## The Rocks

I'm neither geologist nor rockhound, and so I cannot truly tell of the stone treasures of the desert. I admire the mountains because of their grandeur; the massive tapestry of their many-colored cliffs and canyons, their serenity against the sky. But how they came to be, the titanic forces that thrust them up and the millions of years of erosion that slowly brings them down are beyond my comprehension. There are many books on the geology of the Death Valley area; the seeker after wisdom in such matters is referred to them. There are people who can walk the hard black crust left by volcanoes long cold and pick up pretty pebbles—red, black, streaked—that I trudge indifferently over. There are excellent books that tell of where gems may be found. *Desert Gem Trails* by Mary Frances Strong, is a splendid field guide to the gems and minerals of the Mojave and Colorado Deserts, with fine detailed maps of how to get there and what you will find. The nearby El Pasos are a gem seekers delight, and a multiplicity of stones—chalcedony, opal, yellow moss jasper, agate, and such exotic items as zeolite and calcite crystals—are there to be found, although they are getting pretty well picked over by now. (There's supposed to be gold in Iron Canyon, but I personally shoveled seven hundred scoops of sand into my son's dry panner and got a minuscule speck of gold for the work.)

Only one place of stones intrigues me—that open cave at the north end of Last Chance Canyon where, up until a few years ago, symmetrical pillars supported its roof. These were the petrified remains of ancient palm trees which flourished when Black Mountain was an island in a prehistoric swamp. Professional poachers have sawed them off and sold them, but on the slopes in front of the cave there are many fine glassy pieces of petrified palm, some of them a lovely blue with razor sharp edges. It is now forbidden to take these stones.

Because this is a first-hand account, I make no attempt to tell at length of the mineral wealth of the valleys. The western Panamint canyons were rich in gold—Bullfrog and World Beater were two of Shorty Harris' better strikes. At the head of Surprise Canyon once stood Panamint City, now ruins, but then a place of lucrative silver mines. Sometime, if my legs hold out, I hope to hike to the top end of Johnson Canyon (the best of 4WD's can't make it) to the ruins of Hungry Bills Ranch, where, it is said, are the vestiges of old orchards. The borax flats of Death Valley were profitable, and the famous Twenty Mule Team wagons hauled borax the 160 miles to the railhead at Mojave. As a boy in Beverly, Massachusetts, I once looked with awe at the great wide-wheeled rig and its strong mules, sent East as a publicity venture, little knowing I would some time retrace its track by truck. And as I have previously said, it is a cause for reflection to me as I pass by the big dry lakes—Koehn and Searles—and consider that from under these flat, white, and occasionally wet playas, vast automated mills such as the Kerr-Magee plant at Trona, pipe a complex mix of chemicals that bring far more money to stockholders than the romantic gold and silver veins ever brought.

*Death Valley Coyote*

# 11
# The Lure of the Desert

One hot summer afternoon I sat in the wispy shade of a scraggly little aspen at Tuttle Creek Camp just above Lone Pine, weary and sweaty from wrestling with my camper, which for some reason had gone balky and taken 320 strokes to raise instead of the customary 70. I looked across the valley with the thin green crooked line marking the course of the Owens River (the first chosen to quench the voracious thirst of distant thievish Los Angeles) to the long, grim, gray-and-black wall of the Inyo Range rising against the hot blue sky: no trees, no least emerald tracery of a canyon creek, barren hostile hills where no man and few beasts dwell. (No wonder the Japanese in World War II, interned at Manzanar, abandoned hope of escape with such a prison wall before them.)

     I had just come down from a jaunt into the Sierra, where the creeks —Pine, Taboose, Horton, and many others— brim-full of icy water from the deep winter snowpack, rushed with power and great speed down the steep eastern slope into the lush valley. I had been to high Onion Valley where the snow lingered, the road ended, and the trail over Kearsarge Pass began; and to the end of pavement at Pine Creek where the redwoods were tall, the alders green, and the air pine-scented and cool. I was puzzled by my attitude. Why, I asked, should anybody be interested in, fascinated by, the dreary Inyos when such alpine delights could be easily had? What is the nature of the potent lure of the desert and the rocky emptiness of desert ranges? For the Inyos, and Saline and Eureka Valleys which lay behind them, tugged at me with a power the lush and watered slopes of the Sierra Nevada did not have. My mind went back to the lines of Wilfrid Thesiger, who knew this lure and told of it in unmatched words.

Thesiger, who is one of that strange breed of rather mad and incredibly tough men England has produced, wrote what to me is unquestionably the greatest account of desert travels, *Arabian Sands*. James Wellard, in his fine volume, *The Great Sahara*, gives a full list of those who first crossed the immense spaces of that desert begun in 1825 with Major Alexander Laing and Rene Caillie three years later followed by many daring, and sometimes foolhardy explorers—Henry Barth, Daniel Houghton, Mungo Park, Frederick Hornneman, G. F. Lyon, and even Miss Alexandrine Tinne, that pioneer female explorer who was filled with a romantic spirit and went far, only to die young (29), hacked in arm and neck by a Taureg sword and left to bleed to death in the far sands. But these writers wrote accounts of their journeys which were more descriptive than philosophical. Charles Doughty's *Arabia Deserta*, a tale of a bold trip to Mecca by a Christian who would have been instantly killed had his infidel nature been known, does more by way of getting the spirit of the desert than do these others. Lawrence of Arabia, whose *Seven Pillars of Wisdom* should certainly be read, also gets the feel of the desert in a quotation I shall finally cite. (We have one American book which attempts this, Edward Abbey's *Desert Solitaire*. It has passages of perceptive writing, but unfortunately it is to me a mean-spirited book, distilling the worst of the Me Generation into poisoned words. The ugliness of his spirit lies over his clear prose like rattlesnake venom on a glass slide.)

Thesiger's magnificent account tells of two trips he made across the Rub al Kahil—The Empty Quarter in Saudi Arabia. Two white men, Thomas and Philby, had gone before him, but the one was a convert to Islam and thus less in danger from the merciless fanatics of the desert, and the other went an easier route, with more wells. The book is superbly illustrated with black and white plates which present an etched impression of the dune-covered waste that lusher color shots could not match. Thesiger lived for months under almost unbearable conditions, enduring what his Bedu guides endured. You must read the book to get the feel of the terror and emptiness of the Arabian sands; no condensation can do it. In a far more exotic setting, he puts the question that came to me as I looked at the tamer Inyos. He begins the book by writing:

> I first realized the hold the desert had upon me when travelling in the Hajaz Mountains in the summer of 1946 ... For a while I had lived with the Bedu a hard and merciless life; during which I was always hungry and usually thirsty. My companions had

> been accustomed to this life since birth, but I had been wracked by the weariness of long marches through wind-whipped dunes, or across plains where monotony was emphasized by the mirages shimmering through the heat... Hunger, thirst, heat and cold: I had endured them in full in those six months, and had endured the strain of living among an alien people who had no allowance for weakness. Often, in weariness of body and spirit, I had longed to get away.
>
> Now, in the Assir, I was standing on a mountainside forested with wild olives and junipers. A stream tumbled down its slope; its water, ice cold at 9,000 feet, was in welcome contrast with the scanty bitter water of the sands. There were wild flowers, jasmine and honeysuckle, wild roses, pinks and primulas... Far below me a yellow haze hid the desert to the east. Yet it was there my fancies ranged, planning new journeys while I wondered at this strange compulsion which drove me back to a life that was barely possible... But I knew instinctively that it was the very hardness of life in the desert which drew me back there—it was the same pull which takes men back to the polar ice, to high mountains, and to the sea.

And at the risk of over-quoting I must share with you some of the superb prose of Thesiger's Prologue; no man, not even Charles Doughty, has better caught the harsh allure of the desert.

> A cloud gathers, the rain falls, men live; the cloud disperses without rain, and men and animals die. In the deserts of southern Arabia there is no rhythm of the seasons, no rise and fall of sap, but empty wastes where only the changing temperature marks the passages of the year. It is a bitter desiccated land which knows nothing of gentleness or ease. Yet men have lived there since earliest times... they accept hardships and privations; they know no other way... No man can live this life and emerge unchanged. He will carry, however faint, the imprint of the desert, the brand which marks the nomad; and he will have within him the yearning to return, weak or insistent

according to his nature. For this cruel land can cast
a spell which no temperate clime can match.

Thesiger's eloquence spoke strongly to me in my later years, but long before I ever read him or even saw the desert, I was strangely moved by the words of Zane Grey. His novel, *The Wanderer of the Wasteland*, made a mysterious appeal to me while I was still in high school, and indeed I quoted it at length at a youth service in my home Church the first time I ever spoke from a pulpit. His hero, Wansfell, hears an old prospector tell of the harsh enduring realities of the desert which will outlast and consume all the works of man. To be sure, as I later found, Grey laid it on a bit thick: the temperature of Death Valley never reached 140 degrees; there are no such "furnace winds of midnight" as Grey conjures up as a backdrop for his lurid finale. But he used evocative names—the Funeral Range, the Black Mountains, and the Panamints—and I find it exceedingly strange that these names which without reason enthralled me in my teens should have become known realities as I neared my eighties, and should still hold the same irrational magic spell over me. For me the enticement of the desert began long before I ever saw or walked it.

Why do I go to the desert? What, precisely, is its call to me? My wife, who is a Pisces and despises the scorching aridities of the desert and all its attendant dangers and discomforts, once asked me, "Harry, when there are so many smooth roads and wonderful views, why do you seek out these miserable jolting trails?" There is a simple answer—the lure of the desert. But the lure itself is by no means simple. I have read that the perfumes by which women lure men are complex aromas, subtle minglings of many oils and essences. Curiously, some of the most delicate and costly perfumes have as a basic ingredient the glandular secretion of the civet cat, a smell most vile of itself, but which has the property of fixing and holding the more volatile and sweeter flower fragrances. Perhaps it is the very bleakness, the hardness, the lethal potential of desert travel that serves as civet to its complex allurement. At all events, the enticement of the outback is for me an intricate music and among its notes are seldom-seen beauty, the spice of danger, spatial emptiness, solitude, awe, and God. I briefly sound each of these notes.

## 12

## Seldom Seen Beauty

There is much beauty in Death Valley—Dante's View, the yellow convoluted hills below Zabriskie Point, the chromatic profusion of Artist's Palette, and they are all much worth seeing, as is the awesome north-and-south sweep of the great Valley itself—a stunning sight. Every proper visitor sees these things. But I speak of beauty less often viewed and then only at the cost of travelling long miles of empty roads with rocks, sand, mud, scary drop-offs and other impediments to smooth and carefree travel. I have already described some of these beauties in my treatment of the seven valleys. But there is one such place in the big Valley which I must include.

If you will turn off I 15 at Baker, drive north to Wade's Exit, turn right again at the identifying sign, ford the river (as posted, at times it can be tricky and sticky), you will come to the oasis of Saratoga Springs. There, at the southern end of the dryest area of the continent of North America, flanked by the barren Owlshead and Ibex Mountains, are three ponds of fresh water with just a hint of salt in the taste, with acres of green rushes, all manner of aquatic fowl—little birds darting over sheets of glassy water mirroring the clean sky. Saratoga Springs is a cluster of emeralds and turquoise in a setting of brass and iron. Now to some less known but lovely places.

### Cottonwood Canyon

The Cottonwood Canyon jeep trail runs out of Stovepipe Wells and dwindles into a footpath into Saline Valley, so I have been told. I had often wanted to drive up that canyon but didn't dare tackle it alone. One day a friend with more nerve and less experience than I shamed me into trying it. For nine miles we bounced along a wash and turned eastward into the mountains by way of a narrowing canyon. At last he stopped (he was in the lead), not by wisdom but by sheer luck, fifty yards short of deep, dry sand which surely would have trapped him. A post with a sign bearing merely two letters, "C" and "M", told us that we were at the junction of Cottonwood and Marble Canyons. The day was a quiet perfection of desert travel—crystal air, austere loveliness of sun-drenched rocks and shrubs, and sudden creamy clouds sliding swiftly over the high canyon rim. We four ate a pleasant lunch, took pictures, and drove back out of the canyon to see an uncommon and impressive sight—rain storms all over the northern part of Death Valley. Above the slopes and summits of the Cottonwood, the Grapevine, and the Funeral Mountains thick gray veils of rain hung down from the black cloud masses, while parts of the long basin were bright with sunshine. We were safely out of the canyon and in no danger of being caught in a flash flood, and our hearts rejoiced at the dappled splendor of the skies. It had been an uneventful day, no truly exciting scenery, just pleasant companionship in a place where we shared the beauty with no other eyes.

*Owens Dry Lake from Cerro Gordo*

## Cerro Gordo

Out of the dying town of Keeler, once a port from which a steamer carried ore across the twelve-foot-deep Owens Lake, a road runs up into the Inyos to the town of Cerro Gordo (population 2, once 4000) and the now inoperative mine that in its years of operation produced $17,000,000 worth of silver. The mine machinery—steam engines, boilers, generators—is massive, and you wonder how it was ever brought up from the flatlands. The owners are hospitable, and the old hotel is still in reasonably good shape. The owners and the government keep the road graded, but it is extremely steep and narrow and at times there is only a foot of it between your outside wheels and a drop of five hundred feet or more. It's not a good road to meet other traffic on. One morning we stood 8,000 feet up and saw the sun on Owens Dry Lake (Los Angeles has legally stolen its once abundant water), an improbable melange of silver, green, blue, tan, and shades of purple and violet, with the brutal gray escarpment of Olancha Mountain rising behind it. My son said, "There's nothing better in Death Valley."

## Titus Canyon

Go north from Furnace Creek and take the road to Beatty, Nevada. You will come to the one-way Titus Canyon Road. Part of it is so narrow that two cars cannot possibly pass, and it is therefore closed to east-bound traffic. The Auto Club map gives it a jeep trail rating. Actually, it is very easy driving, but deep in the canyon it is awesome to look up at the sheer cliffs that tower 500 feet almost perpendicularly a couple of feet on either side. Seen from the bottoms of such canyons the sky is always an intense dark blue, and I have heard it said that from the bottom of a deep well you can see the stars at noonday. A party of us went through Titus Canyon when storm clouds were gathering over the Grapevine Peaks. The view was worrisome, but exciting. The rain held off till we reached hard surface. For me the most memorable thing about Titus Canyon was the contrast between the ghost town of Leadfield, located in an opening halfway through, and the rosy romance of a faded promotional poster. In the Twenties an unscrupulous promoter salted some rocks, announced that he had made a rich strike, called the site Leadfield, and pushed the sale of the mine stock to gullible Easterners. Only those who have travelled the waterless wastes of that region can fully appreciate the wild humor of that faded chromolithograph. It depicted a big steamboat which had navigated the dry wash of the Amargosa River (nearly 300 miles from tidewater), steamed a hundred miles up Death Valley, the dryest spot in America, sailed up a canyon to an altitude of 4,000 feet, and there lowered its gangplank to permit its passengers—ladies in ankle-length dresses and big floppy hats, gentlemen in natty straw hats and blazers—to set foot in the imaginary bustling boom town. Actually the defrauded investors did not collect a nickle's worth of lead or any other ore, and in a short year the town died, leaving rusty, drab, uninspiring ruins.

## Aguereberry Point

I am enchanted by this coign of vantage, not only because of the view from it, but because there is a fine story concerning it. Dante's View in the Black Mountains on the east side of Death Valley is the place to view the Valley in the morning; it is much visited and deservedly so. But on the west side, a bit to the north, on a jutting buttress in the Panamints, Aguereberry Point is the afternoon place of seeing.

I first viewed it under ideal conditions. It was near sunset and a thunderstorm was brewing to the west. The sun's low golden beams shot through openings in the boiling masses of clouds—purple, gray, smoky white with gilded edges—and lighted up the cliffs and canyons of the Funeral Mountains twenty miles across the valley; their colors were black, ochre, yellow, all tinged with an aureate luminescence, and the green groves of Furnace Creek were plain to see in the strange slanting light. As the light abruptly lessened I turned from contemplation of the eastern splendor and looked west. A great splash of late sunlight shone on the green graben of Emigrant Pass, and a strong flash of jagged white lightning slashed the inky storm front; not for ten seconds did the thunder roll. The storm was only two miles away, but the rain never came.

The trail to the Point from the Trona-Wildrose Road is sharply angular and narrow, but not dangerous, and it is this trail that sets Aguereberry point apart from all other view points. The roads to them were built by public funds; not so with this trail. Pete Aguereberry was a Basque sheepherder turned prospector. In his search for gold he came to the point, and was so taken by the noble sight that all by himself, with pick, shovel, and cart, he hewed out a rough road to the hitherto inaccessible buttress so that others might feast on the beauty that had fed his soul. How fine a deed that was! How esthetic, how noncommercial! I think of the men of multiple millions—Carnegie, Frick, Ford, Huntington Hartford, Hearst, Norton Simon, J. Paul Getty, and others who at great cost in coin have made things of beauty available in famous museums and collections. But this man who earned a scant subsistence by scratching the hard hills for gold, gave greatly of his imagination, muscle, toil, and benevolence to make it possible for his fellow men to bless their eyes with rare beauty. The beauty he possibilized was greater than gold, and more lasting. My name for him is Pete Aguereberry, patron of the arts.

# 13

# The Spice of Danger

**A**nd I mean only a dusting of that spice. I personally am not up to the hard runs true off-roaders make; too old, too little mechanical aptitude. The macho-type off-roaders welcome fiendish stretches of incredible difficulty. Events like the Silverstone Run, the Sierra Trek, the Poker Run, the Jeepers' Jamboree, the Rubicon Trail, are held in the high mountains over terrain that seems to the uninitiated eye to be utterly impassable. But the trips are made by groups of skilled drivers with guides to show the way along some of the narrow, tilted trails, and huge rocks. Ordinary 4WDs are not permitted on some of these jaunts; only specialized machines with huge tires, potent winches, high clearance, short wheelbase, pairs of heavy duty shocks on each wheel, great gobs of torque—such trailmasters as the Jeep CJs, the Toyota FJ 40s, Land Rover 88s, and the like. But in such runs the danger is more to gear than to persons; there's always help at hand.

Nor do I have reference to the sort of peril incurred in famous runs in far places. The first of these, I suppose, was the great around-the-world race in 1909 which was won by the Thomas Flyer. The very machine that made it is still on display at Harrah's Club in Reno, Nevada. It's a superb still life; the gallant old machine, high-wheeled, of immense engine, bits of the original ropes tied onto the front bumper, and the crew of three, in goggles and long dusters, facing the bitter winds of Siberia. What men they must have been—no top, no windshield, no garages, and often no roads. And they were strangers in a strange land. In these days there is still the Alaska-Patagonia run through Latin America. In the 1920s Citroen proved that their trucks could cross the Sahara in convoy, and legend has it that an American, taking seriously Ford's advertising of long ago—"No hill too steep; no sand too deep"—took a trio of modified Model Ts far into the wastes of Morroco or Libya. The perils such safaris encountered are not those of which I am to speak.

The dangers you will encounter in the California outback are distinctly minor and can be lessened almost to the vanishing point. A common peril is getting stuck. This can be avoided by simple techniques. The first of these is to have a well-tuned car, checking everything before you hit the dirt. If you can't do it yourself, take it to your garage. Be sure that your wires, tubes, hoses, and the like are in good shape. Check your oil, water, and tires. Mini-trucks and many passenger cars are capable of taking some very bad roads if they are in tune. If you go in a passenger car the great factor of concern is clearance—how many inches of empty space do you have between the lowest point of your machine's viscera and the surgically-sharp rocks of a desert or canyon road? A simple and successful technique of remaining unstuck is prudence. If you come to a doubtful place, don't charge into it. Get out and walk ahead, and if you can't make it, employ creative cowardice. Don't try it.

For it must be remembered that equipment alone cannot ensure desert safety; the driver must help. Too often enthusiastic novices buy fine 4WDs, take them to the outback on the first free weekend and get ignominiously or dangerously stuck. A greenhorn with the best of rig will bog down where a skilled, desert-wise driver will get through with a lesser vehicle. Prepare yourself as well as your truck. Make your first trips in the company of experienced back country people. Read the many available books and brochures on off-road travel. Subscribe to one of the off-road magazines; their articles are informative. *Off-Road*, for example, in its July 1981 issue, has an excellent piece, "Going Solo," which deals with the hazards of the outback and how to minimize them. The Subaru people put out a splendid manual of off-road driving basics—"Getting Dirty." Join a 4WD club, or, if you are a loner, as I am, use common sense and caution. Given a sound, well-maintained car or truck, you are the key factor in keeping out of trouble.

Further, your truck or car should be well-equipped. Be sure you have an abundance of water. A gallon a day per person is a good rule of thumb. Extra gas, oil, are essential, and such things as brake fluid and an air pump are advisable. You should also carry a shovel and a tow rope; perhaps for another, perhaps for yourself. True aficionados carry a high-lift jack and perhaps a winch. Extra food is a good idea, but I have never used any of my emergency rations. It's assumed that you will have your meals planned ahead for the length of your stay. There are many desirable extras. You ought to have detailed maps of the area in your glove compartment: the Auto Club supplies them to members, and the Bureau of Land Management gives them away. Indeed, the Bureau has a superb little brochure, "Off-Road Vehicle Recreation," which is lush with color shots and rich with detailed suggestions for back country behavior and fun.

If you make it a habit to hit the dirt seriously, you'll soon have your rig full of desirable gear—a tool box, first aid kit, bug repellent, lip ice, sun tan lotion, paper towels, and the like. The complete inventory for my truck is so lengthy that it takes two single-spaced pages to name each item and tell its place of storage. A comfort in the heat is a big cooler with solid ice (cubes melt too fast), and at all times a good propane stove with a big fuel container is desirable. There's little natural fuel in the desert and in most places it's unlawful to use it. Bring your own wood for a campfire. If you are just going to take an exploratory trip or two to the outback, you don't need a multiplicity of gear. But you must have the basics—vehicle in good condition, extra gas and oil, water, warm clothing—the essentials of survival. For while the chances are high that if you drive sensibly your trip will be without accident or hardship, there's always the possibility that suddenly, through foul luck or chance of weather, you may find yourself in a survival situation.

When I was sailing, I was given two pieces of advice that apply to desert driving. The first was, "Don't leave your boat and swim for shore." The other was, "Be sure you have a jug of water and a big box of crackers." From all that I have read and heard, the most serious danger in desert travel is leaving a car that is out of gas or broken down and trying to walk for help. There are exceptions to this general rule, of course; water or help may be a known distance away; but ordinarily desert distances are too big for walking to be anything but perilous, especially in hot weather. No summer goes by but that the Los Angeles papers carry the news that people, even experienced desert people, have died of thirst in walking out for help. The safe doctrine is to stay by your truck as the swamped sailor stayed by his boat. Help will finally come even on the most lonesome road; be sure you have the food and fluids to make waiting merely uncomfortable, not lethal. And, of course, it is the part of wisdom (although I personally seldom do it) to let somebody know where you are going and when you expect to return. Volumes have been written about safe travel in the desert. A key element in outback safety is to be over-prepared. Carry more than you may need of gas, water, food, clothing, spare gear. "Better to have it and not use it, than to need it and not have it."

There is, of course, one type of deadly accident which can happen in back country driving, but which in fact doesn't often occur—the fall off a narrow trail into a deep canyon. During the Christmas holidays in 1982 three people died from such falls in the snowy San Gabriels. They had gotten out of their cars, slipped on snow, and fallen off the edge of an Angeles Forest road. What the drop left undone, below-zero temperatures and the unavoidable slowness of rescue finished. It is scary to look out of the passenger-side window on a narrow trail and see hundreds of feet of emptiness just under your right elbow. I once took a party up to Pinon Ridge for a cocktail party simply for the sheer silliness of it, arguing that probably nothing like that had happened in the long geological life of that ridge of noble view. One woman in the party was terrified at the ride up and had to have several stiff ones to fortify her for the return trip. (For the benefit of sober-minded people I record that none of the drivers lifted a glass.) I have sometimes wondered if a loss of control or a break-away of the edge might be the machinery of my trip to the Promised Land. But since death finally comes to all men, I would prefer the few seconds of horror on the way down to the shattering rocks as a means of exit from this world to the far slower and more ugly process I have seen in pastoral calls at what are euphemistically called "rest homes."

But, as I have said, the chief danger is leaving a stalled car and starting to walk for help. The great hot valleys are no place for pedestrians. I once saw an old photograph circa 1931, which showed a heap of stones mounded over the final stopping place of Val Nolan, with a crudely lettered marker—"A victim of the elements." Sometimes, driving along in 110 degree heat, a wet towel sitting over my shoulders to provide the delicious chill of evaporation, or sitting at twilight in contemplation, looking out over the gray flatlands to the dark mountains, I have pondered over the theological problem posed by the terrible moral neutrality of nature. For nature is indifferent to human virtue or wickedness, and will impartially starve, dehydrate, or freeze gross villain or near-saint. Neither agonized prayers, bitter blasphemies, nor stoic submission alter the inexorable doom of "a victim of the elements." Jesus notes this fact in the Sermon on the Mount, for sun and rain take no account of the goodness or badness of the people they descend upon. But I have not heard a sermon (save one I once delivered myself) upon the perplexing thought that the fearful moral indifference of nature is not due to the mindless mechanisms of the impersonal natural order, but by direction of God, himself, our heavenly Father; for it is he, says Christ, who eliminates the factor of just treatment in nature's functioning.

> ... For he maketh his sun to rise upon the evil and on
> the good, and sendeth rain upon the just and unjust.

The text can be justified, I suppose, by the belief that sun and rain are there considered to be the beneficent agents of growth and harvest. But the desert philosopher, seeing the lethal power of the murderous sun, and what either drought or flash flood can do, reads the familiar verse with a touch of chill.

There is one sort of danger to be found in lonely places which is more a matter of imagination or remote chance than of high probability. At one time these areas were places of the peril from evil or murderous men. I think it is a very light risk nowadays. To be sure the time was when this was outlaw country. During the 1870s Panamint City was of such evil reputation that Wells Fargo refused to service the town, and 90 years later, when Manson-type hippies and Hell's Angels-style bikers were roaming about seeking whom they might hassle, the peril of robbery or death was not to be taken lightly. But this sort of thing seems to have lessened in recent years, and certainly the back country at night is safer than the streets of Los Angeles. I always carry a hand gun, as most of my acquaintances do, more for the sense of security it gives than for actual use against marauders. Many experts hold that the mere appearance of a gun is a sufficient deterrent; it doesn't have to be fired. Some years ago a pistol manufacturer ran a vivid ad. It portrayed a lonely rider by his campfire, his horse picketed nearby. The text was something like this. "Nightfall ... solitude ... the crack of a twig ... your Colt ... confidence." When I am making dry camp in the outback, alone or with a single companion, if a strange sound wakens me, I am not wholly ill at ease, for my hand can curl around the checkered walnut butt of my big .45. I once was fleet of foot and strong of arm. I am not so now, but that potent gun is a very long arm, a very hard fist, and by it, if worst came to desperate worst, I could give an account of myself.

So much for the whiff of the spice of danger. It isn't a strong seasoning, but it gives a piquancy to travel in the back country.

# 14

# Emptiness and Solitude

Emptiness and solitude are the two sides of a coin of reality. It is not wholly accurate to name one the obverse and the other the reverse; this implies that one is superior to the other. Emptiness, as I shall use the term, is the physical absence of mankind. Solitude is the aloneness of the individual man. And while solitude can theoretically take place in the midst of a crowd, it is more easily attained, I shall argue, in the emptiness of the desert.

    I'm not going to talk of emptiness on the cosmic scale. Astronomers tell us that despite the bewildering multiplicity of planets and stars, so great is the universe that there are enormous distances of empty space between these bodies. I really can't grasp some of the figures the astronomers give us; they benumb my conceiving. I remember once telling the youngsters at Church of the Messiah a comparison I picked up somewhere to the effect that if the earth was a speck of dust in our chancel, the sun was an orange in Palm Springs 110 miles away. That's about the limit of my comprehension. More startling illustrations are available, but when learned men begin talking about parsecs, googols, and googolplexes, they have soared beyond my dull wits. A parsec is 19.2 billion miles. "Googol" is a word invented by the American mathematician Edward Kasner for dealing with great magnitudes. It is the numeral 1 followed by 100 zeroes. Even more ungraspable is the "googolplex"— a googol of googols, or the figure 10 raised to the power googol. I once read that it would take a sizeable book, with the first letter an arabic 1, with many, many pages of zeroes to give a googolplex numerical expression. A googolplex is the largest possible finite number.

I'm not going to talk about the space between the molecules in what looks to be solid matter. Only the dwarf stars are really packed, they have such enormous magnetic pull that even light can't get away, thus forming black holes. If they get small enough they crush themselves to death, and come out into a new life as a blazing new star in a sort of resurrection from the dead.

All this, I say, is rather beyond me, and I find the midget magnitudes of earth (if such an oxymoron can stand) impressive enough. Emptiness has a powerful fascination, and it need not be of the desert sand; snow and water can have the same effect. The white arctic wastes are spiritually moving in their emptiness. Knud Rasmussen, the Danish explorer, quotes Ikjugaruuk, a Caribou Eskimo:"All true wisdom is only to be found far from the dwellings of men, in the great solitudes, and it can only be attained through suffering. Suffering and privation are the only things that can open the mind of man to that which is hidden from his fellows." I find in this profound observation a relationship to the life and death of Christ, for we know that when he was in need of wisdom he departed into a desert place to pray, and in the lonely suffering of the cross he was made perfect.

Water also can give the awesome sensation of emptiness. The expanse of ocean, even when seen from a beach, can move people and inspire poets—"Roll on, thou deep and dark blue ocean, roll." But nowhere in literature is the impact of emptiness on man better described than in that passage in *Moby Dick*, where Melville, the American Shakespeare, tells what it did to Pip, the little black slave, who was left behind in the chase of a whale. Stubb, the third mate, had warned Pip that if he jumped out of the boat again (he had already cost the ship a $3,000 whale) he would not be picked up.

> It was a beautiful, bounteous, blue day; the spangled sea calm and cool, and flatly stretching away, all around, to the horizon... Bobbing up and down in that sea, Pip's ebon head showed like a head of cloves... In three minutes, a whole mile of shoreless ocean was between Pip and Stubb. Out from the centre of the sea, poor Pip turned his crisp, curling black head to the sun, another castaway, though the loftiest and brightest.
>
> Now in calm weather, to swim in the open ocean is as easy to the practised swimmer as to ride in a spring-carriage ashore. But the awful lonesomeness is intolerable. The intense concentration of self in

> the middle of such a heartless immensity, my God! who can tell it? Mark, now when sailors in a dead calm bathe in the open sea—mark how closely they hug their ship and only coast along her sides.
>
> But had Stubb really abandoned the poor little negro to his fate? No, he did not mean to, at least. Because there were two boats in his wake, and he supposed, no doubt, that they would of course come up to Pip very quickly, and pick him up... But it so happened, that those boats, without seeing Pip, suddenly spying whales close to them on one side, turned, and gave chase: and Stubb's boat was now so far away, and he and all his crew so intent upon his fish, that Pip's ringed horizon began to expand about him miserably. By the merest chance, the ship itself at last rescued him; but from that hour the little negro went about the deck an idiot... The sea had jeeringly kept his finite body up, but drowned the infinite of his soul.

Great land expanse without inhabitants can have emotional and spiritual impact. California is a big state, with much unoccupied real estate, but its population density is greater than that of Alaska, which has but one person in two square miles. Yet these are thickly populated areas compared to the Northwest Territory of Canada, which provides 28 square miles for each person to roam in. Robert Service, the poor man's Kipling, catches the mood these spaces generated in the sourdough goldseeker in his poem which begins

> Were you ever out in the Great Alone
> When the moon was awful clear?

(In case some persnickety person objects to snow and water as being incongruous qualities in a desert, let me remind you that while we think of deserts as sandy, etymologically, a desert is a place where nobody, or few people live; it is a deserted area and the nature of its surface is irrelevant.) The Mojave, which takes in Death Valley and many arid valleys of Southern California, is not as empty as Alaska or the watery wastes of the Canadian Northwest Territories, but it is big enough to give the solitary back country trucker or hiker a lonesome feeling by day or night.

Emptiness can be exhilarating or terrifying. When you take the new road over Sherman Pass and look over the Kern Plateau, seeing the back sides of Olancha and Whitney, the unhoused space, the clean air, and the wide sky enlarge your soul. You see why Joaquin Miller makes California demand

> Men to match my mountains.

But empty space can frighten; witness the pioneer women who went mad with cabin fever—the psychic malaise that smote the solitary wife in her isolated cabin on the endless Dakota plains. Hardened mountain men spoke of "seeing the elephant"—the eerie phantom that struck terror to the soul of the lonely trapper by his campfire and sent him shaken back to civilization. The Greeks had a striking proverb: "See Pan, and die." Pan was the god of nature, and nature was not a pleasant blend of flowers, birds, and rippling springs; it was harsh, lethally intimidating, and the lone Greek shepherd in Arcadia who saw the goat-god, was as terror-smitten as the mountain man who saw the impossible fire-eyed pachyderm in the Rockies. Aristotle says that great drama should result in a catharsis—a cleansing or purging of the soul by pity and terror. In its extreme manifestations, the emptiness of pitiless nature is unmitigated terror.

Emptiness is a kind of infinity, and while finite man needs something of it in his cramped life, too much of it is overwhelming. Infinity has two dimensions in art; the vertical and the horizontal. The soaring height of a Gothic nave gives to kneeling men and women a sense of the infinitude of God, and this is usually comforting. But I recall one odd episode when, for some reason I cannot wholly fathom, the cathedral-inspired sense of vertical infinity frightened me. Through a train window I first saw the thin gray finger of Salisbury Cathedral (my favorite) pointing up through the rain as I stopped at the station on my way to Cornwall. It fascinated me, and, on my next trip to England, I paid a day's visit to that prayer in stone. It was a cold May day with a strong wind blowing low clouds at high speed. I walked all around the edifice until I came to a place where the western transept joined the nave and looked up, standing close to the stone. The spire is the tallest in England, 408 feet, and as I looked at its lofty tip, the racing clouds, which seemed barely to graze it, gave the illusion that the spire was toppling over on me. I told myself it was foolishness. To be sure, Christopher Wren had dropped lead and plumb line inside and found the steeple 28½ inches out of true. But this did not account for the inescapable and terrifying conviction that the great gray column was falling over on me. So strong was the fear that I had to leave the spot.

Fifty years or so ago I read a book which had a lasting effect upon my intellectual life. It was Rudolph Ott's masterly volume, *Das Heileger*—The Idea of the Holy. In it Otto makes the now familiar distinction between two essential parts of God's nature: the *mysterium tremendum*—the great mystery which awes and repels—and the *fascinans*—the sweetness and light that attracts and endears. The second of these elements was familiar enough to me, for I had been reared in a Baptist Church where the love of God was warmly preached. The first, the realization that God is a being of power and mystery, to be approached with fear and trembling, was new, and the effect was good. For one thing it kept me from getting cozy with God, and spared me the sickening inanity of the "Hi, God! How ya' doin'?" mode of worship which sullies many sanctuaries in these slovenly times. (I can't accept the present practice of addressing God in public worship with the familiar second person "you." In private intimate devotions such address is appropriate, but not in the dignity of public worship. He is "Thee" and "Thou" to me, and I stubbornly mutter these to myelf when the bulletin unison prayer calls for "You." Fortunately, the Lord's Prayer has been spared this desacralization, and it is still "Thy will be done."

Well, the emptiness of the desert has both these elements, for there is that about the desert, as I have many times said (and indeed is the theme of this section) which does lure and call. But there is also the sometime crushing awareness of the merciless nature of physical reality: Its vastness, its moral neutrality, its indifference, not only to human life and values, but to all organic life. Out of this awareness comes the sense of two values man should have in the face of the natural order and before God who has made it—awe and wonder. Of which more later.

Solitude I have defined as the aloneness of the individual man. As a life-long condition this is something people cannot bear, for, as the Lord said, "It is not good that the man should be alone; I will make him a helpmeet for him." (Genesis 2:18). But as any long-married man or woman can witness, total togetherness can be too much of a good thing. In the whole experience of living there come times when the silence of solitude is sweeter than the sound of the dearest voice, when the touch of the most gentle or most amorous hand is less desirable than the almost impalpable brushing of the soft desert air. We need solitude to offset the physically, socially, psychically crowded condition of life in our time. Now it is true that people can be alone in a crowd; one of Thomas Wolfe's most poignant lines is that "loneliness is the prevailing weather of man's soul." But I hold that such loneliness is the result of a misanthropic outlook on life. He who is friendly toward others will always find companionship, not as much of it as he would like, perhaps, and not always when he wants it. But the man or woman who lives for others will know less loneliness than the aloof or selfish soul. Of course, in the big picture, in the hard reality of man's sojourn in this world of time, each of us is twice alone, once as he enters it and once as he leaves it; birth and death are lonely happenings.

What I am talking about, however, is the need for some solitude in the social press of urban life. Spatial emptiness is one way to spacious interior life. Wordsworth is profoundly right when he says

> The world is too much with us; late and soon,
> Getting and spending, we lay waste our powers...

We need physical social space in order to get the spiritual aloneness which is necessary for maturation. Some years ago I read of a scientist, Swedish, I think, who conducted an experiment of hard meaning. He took a given number of rats and put them in a large cage in which each rat had a certain amount of space. The rats flourished, gave birth, fought minimally, and kept a rattish sanity. Then into the selfsame space he introduced an additional number of rodents. Nothing else was changed—food, water, air quality. In months the colony was literally a madhouse; the rats fought murderously, the females stopped bearing, diseases multiplied. Only one thing had been altered: the amount of space alloted each rat. Now since rats are more like humans than any other beasts (they are omnivorous, eating what is there to eat; have no rutting season, but mate all the year round; and they have racial prejudices—white, brown, gray, and black rats will fight for no other reason than for color), social lessons are to be learned from human-like *rattus rattus* and his kind. It's not a matter of economics alone; when the density of human population goes up, so does crime and insanity, in affluent suburb as well as in the poverty-stricken ghetto. There can be subtler manifestations of the lack of room around each living entity. If five members of a family live in reasonable harmony, discord can come when divorced sister Jane and her child come home to live for a while. Be the family as friendly as it may, the mood will deteriorate; space is a spiritual necessity.

The quality of life is lessened by too many people in too small a space. Mystic Thomas á Kempis puts it well, "The more I walked among men, the less of a man I became." Even devout men, seeking to find God, are hampered by proximity. And it is all but trite to point out that Jesus, whenever the crowd pressure got too great, used to go out to a solitary place to pray. For most people that kind of emptiness is hard come by. It's a long ride to the outback, and our herd living, the mind-set of our times, makes people equate solitude with loneliness and fear. It is an extremely tangled business. The relationship of the individual to the community is one of tremendous importance and complexity. John Donne is, of course, right, "No man is an island" and to be Robinson Crusoe perpetually is impossible; the individual must have a support system. But on the other hand, when Greta Garbo, the moody Swedish beauty, said to Hollywood reporters, "I want to be alone," she was stating a true and deep need of the soul.

I sometimes personally go to the desert because in its emptiness I find a good, soul-satisfying solitude. I couldn't live the solitary life for long, but without a saving salt of solitude, life would lose some of its savor for me. The elements of awe and wonder engendered by the emptiness of the desert are for me essential factors of my religious experience. And the *mysterium tremendum*, the great mystery, the Wholly Other of God as experienced in the natural order, is softened and made bearable by my faith in the love and care of God, the *fascinans*.

In 1956 I had a counter-conversion in my psychological viewpoint. I had been a good Freudian and had read much in his works. But in that year a centennial lecture was given in Beverly Hills by Robert Welder, a leading Freudian. It was an intellectually impressive gathering; a listener without the cloak of a Ph.D. felt naked. But in the course of his lecture, Dr. Welder quoted Freud to this effect: "Some people believe that the experience of the greatness of the natural universe is an ultimate religious experience; to me, it is the ultimate irreligious experience." Instantly my inner weather of psychological climate turned around. This was true atheism, a deep denial of God. The common thought is that Freud was read out of the Jewish world community because of his brutally realistic assessment of Moses in his iconoclastic work, *Moses and Monotheism*, but there is a sense in which Freud's cosmic outlook is totally alien to a faith which produced a poet who could write

> The heavens declare the glory of God, and
> the firmament sheweth his handiwork.

From then on I became a follower of Carl Gustav Jung, who had a place for God in his philosophy of life.

# 15

# God

For me, the final factor of the lure of the desert is finding God. I am not, of course, making the foolish claim that God is only to be found in the desert, or that he is known there more truly than in any other place of encounter. How shall I find thee? Let me count the ways, a lover of God might say, paraphrasing Elizabeth. He has been found in multitudinous places and fashions: in bed as a little child as mother teaches him his "Now-I-lay-me," in Church School as a volunteer teacher tells of old, old stories; in Church, perhaps by Scripture reading or prayer, or the hearing of a hymn, by a sermonic thrust, or by the way in which a soprano's curls catch the chancel light. Men and women have come to know him because they have cried out at midnight and heard an answer, because of the example of parents, or through faith in somebody else's faith. Philosophers have found him because the tortuous paths of thought have led to him; astronomers because the stars they study demand a Creator; mathematicians because they have found that order is heaven's first law, and the ultimate equation of reality is incomplete without an Orderer. Saints and mystics have climbed the ladder of prayer; simpler souls have found him in the common round. And there are those who have never been aware of the moment of discovery because for them he was always there.

Such rhetoric could be dragged out to the point of weariness; the finding of God is a business of infinite variety. The point I repeat here is that our three great Western religions—Judaism, Christianity, and Islam—are desert-bred. Moses, Jesus, and Muhammad were all sons of the desert. What we know as Judaism did not begin with antediluvian patriarchs; it started on the slopes of a desert mountain far south on the Sinai

Peninsula where Moses, that renegade Egyptian in exile because of a killing, was tending sheep for his father-in-law, a Midianite priest.

> Now Moses kept the flock of Jethro his father in law, the priest of Midian: and he led the flock to the backside of the desert, and came to the mountain of God, even to Horeb. And the angel of the Lord appeared unto him in a flame of fire out of the midst of the bush: and he looked, and, behold, the bush burned with fire, and the bush was not consumed. And Moses said, I will now turn aside, and see this great sight, why the bush is not burnt.

Moses, turning aside to see that heavenly fire at closer range, was given the true and great name of God, and Judaism came to be. Our own faith came out of this desert experience; we are sons and daughters of the Judeo-Christian tradition. John the Baptist was the first link between the old and the new. He preached in the desert of Judea, a man after the manner of that other wilderness prophet, Elijah, clothed in camel's hair, eating locusts and wild honey, the scant fare of the desert, a voice crying in the desert, "Prepare ye the way of the Lord." After Jesus was baptized, he did not go to learned rabbis and the written word of God to get the seal of Messiahship. He was driven into the desert by the Spirit for that mighty confontation with Satan, the Enemy. For forty days and forty nights he fasted in the emptiness until he was ready to come into Galilee preaching the gospel of the kingdom of God.

I have written elsewhere: "When the Jews came out of the desert, not for them were the carnal, voluptuous, fertility cults of Canaan. Yahweh dwelt in the high and lonely places; their thought of Him was drained of sensuality and time. He was austere, eternal, terrible as the endless sands and the tall snowless summits of Sinai, Kadesh-Barnea, and Nebo. The God who revealed himself to Moses in a burning bush behind Nebo was not flesh, but spirit."

I find difficulty in keeping from rambling on about the idea of God as variously seen by the Greeks and the Jews. In seminary I was taught that the Hebrew concept of God was anthropomorphic, anthropopathic; God was in the form of a man and had the feelings of a man. The Greeks had a more intellectual concept; their philosophers developed the idea of God as pure impersonal being; God was the *Primum Mobile*, the Unmoved Mover. This is no place to follow the development of God from the minor tribal diety of the Midianites, storm god of the desert mountain, to the lofty and loving Being the great prophets revealed. It's a long leap from the God seen in Joshua's murderous annihilation of the city of Ai to the God who gives Jeremiah the New Covenant—a truth so noble that two millenia after its revelation it is still far beyond men. And of God, Maker of heaven and earth, Father of our Lord Jesus Christ, too much has been well and truly written and preached for me to echo it here.

But I must cock an eyebrow in the direction of the New England Transcendentalists, Thoreau being my particular target, for while they rejected the God of Congregational Calvinism, they were in awe of the Bhagavad Gita and Homer. Hinduism, for all its worth, in actual practice, became a belief in a swarming crawl of proliferated godlets and tree nymphs. The actual working faith of the Greeks of Homer's time (if there really was a single Homer) showed a psychological reaction from the inhuman philosophical exaltation of the Godhead. I have recently been reading the *Illiad*, and the Trojan war as seen in those rolling lines is but the actions of splendid puppets, moved by the lusts and angers of Olympian beings who are merely magnified men and women, but lacking the love and kindness of humans.

So I leave this amateur theological speculation to tell a favorite story. It is from another great desert book, *The Seven Pillars of Wisdom*, Lawrence of Arabia's account of the action in the Middle East during the First World War. Lawrence and his Bedouins conducted raids on the Turkish railway from Medina to Damascus. In one marvelous passage Lawrence tells how two Bedouins took him by moonlight to a ruined castle of a long-dead Persian king, and led him through the rooms of the palace. Entering a room with crumbling walls, they said, "When this room was made, violets were mixed with the clay." And sure enough, said Lawrence, with imagination you could catch the ghost of perfume in the empty hall. "And this wall was made of mud with rose petals." Again the faint memory of flowers. "And this with jasmine." Finally they led him to the broken battlements facing emptiness, and from across nine hundred miles of desert came the clean night wind. "This is the best smell of all," they said.

It is understandable that Arabian mathematicians, products of a desert culture, should have made the discovery of the numeral zero, that immensely important integer. As no smell is the best smell, so no number is the greatest number. In my sketchy study of mysticism, I was impressed by the concept of the *via negavita*, the way of negation, as taught by St. John of the Cross and by that nameless master of the inner life who called himself Dionysius the Areopagite. Their basic idea was that God was essentially unknowable. Man could only know what God was not. In that complex book, *The Cloud of Unknowing*, Dionysius taught that

God dwelt in "dazzling darkness" and the eye of reason could not penetrate it. Centuries later Emerson said much the same thing in his "Bohemian Hymn."

> In many forms we try
> To utter God's infinity.
> But the boundless hath no form,
> And the Universal Friend
> Doth as far transcend
> An angel as a worm.
> The great idea baffles wit,
> Reason staggers under it,
> It leaves the learned in the lurch;
> Nor art, nor power, nor toil can find
> The measure of the Eternal Mind
> Nor hymn, nor prayer, nor Church.

This may be pretty thin stuff for some hearers, and such can sympathize with the stark affirmation of the Jehovah's Witnesses, "God is a being with body, parts, and passions." Many Christians have solved the problem of God's ineffability, his not-ness, by declaring with Paul that he is to be seen in the face of Jesus Christ. For my own part, in my deepest moments, while I hear God as a voice, I see nothing, nor can I conceive of the God who is the maker of heaven and earth as existing in the form of a man, or in any shape, for that matter. But, to get back to the theme of this section, in the emptiness of the desert I find a unique hint of the nature of God. True, the desert experience of God is but a page in the great book of the totality of revelation, but it belongs in the book, and is not the least chapter.

# 16

# For Beginners

Some who read this book might like a taste of the desert, without wanting to take the time and get the gear needed for long jaunts in the outback. You'll need at least $12,000 for a suitable rig at present prices, and you must arrange many days off from work, and find suitable companions. This is a difficult combination to complete, so I am going to suggest a mini-tour which can be done in your car, all on hard surface, adding little time to your west-east or east-west trip from or to California.

I first offer a short side jaunt which will give you a hint of the experience of desert travel—heat (or clean chill depending on the season), dryness, great space, intense light, and stillness. You are driving west on Inter-State Highway 40 to visit your children in Los Angeles. About 30 miles beyond Needles you will come to an intersection called Mountain Springs Summit; there turn south to what is now called National Trails Highway. It's actually old Route 66, the great highway for both Okies and the affluent who were west-bound in the Thirties, Forties, and Fifties. It's strange to see weeds growing out of the cracks on the shoulders, and think that this all-but-empty road was once a crowded transcontinental route.

You'll go through near-ghost towns like Essex and Amboy, and rejoin I 40 at Ludlow, where you can stop for a moment, if you wish, and look at the crumbling edifice of the Ludlow Mercantile Exchange, which in 1908 was a great shopping center for the desert dwellers. As you drive, you'll see range after range of jagged desert mountains—Paiute, Clipper Ship, Marble, and Bullion, along with Bristol Dry Lake and Amboy Crater. If you are interested enough you can read, by way of preparation, John

Steinbeck's *Grapes of Wrath*, and during the long miles in your comfortable car, secure with your credit cards and cash, you may think of the migrant Joads crossing this expanse at night (the heat of day was too great) in an old battered, overloaded truck, poor, patched tires, and no money for food—the truck had to have gas. This detour will not add more than forty-five minutes to your driving time to Los Angeles, but it will show you something of the desert you won't quite see from the freeway. If you are going back to Iowa to visit Aunt Jane, you can reverse directions and take old 66 east from Ludlow.

The second trip I propose is much better for getting the true feel of the desert. It, too, is all over paved road; it will add two to three hours to your journey. You are going east on I 10. Just after the Palm Springs turn-off, take Route 62, and go north through Morongo Valley and east past Twenty-nine Palms. (If you wish, you can follow 62 east all the way to the Colorado River, but I suggest an alternative which will bring you back onto I 10 again.) Not far out of Twenty-nine Palms, you will run through some typical desert terrain; the lunar landscape of the eastern Mojave. I use the adjective "lunar" because it actually does look like the surface of the moon. The mountains are so low and water so scarce that there is absolutely no vegetation on the steep eroded sides of the red and brown hills; not a trace of verdure except on the gently sloping talus soberly clad with dusty, dull-green creosote bushes and mesquite. To your right will be the gray of the Pinto Mountains, to your left the Sheephole Mountains. The aridities of Dale Dry Lake and the sand dunes will cause you to wonder why people settled there. (The lure of gold was the big reason.)

As you top low Clark's Pass, the superb emptiness of Cadiz Valley will open before you, olive and tan under the immense blue sky and glaring white sun, divided by the thin black pencil mark of road stretching far ahead. Stop somewhere out there. Get out of your air-conditioned car and take the hit of the heat. Walk up a dry wash; hear the whisper of sand under your feet; experience the paradoxical singing silence of the desert on a windless day; sense the solitude, the bigness. Don't walk too far from your car, especially in summer; dehydration is a sneaky thing. I once saw my wife collapse simply walking from the car to the edge of the clear poisonous liquid at Bad Water in Death Valley. And I should add that while State 62 is a reasonably well-travelled route, it would do no harm to have a gallon of water in the trunk and a cooler with a couple of six packs of whatever pleases you. You can soon get uncomfortably thirsty, even on this easy loop.

Get back in your car now, and drive on to the junction of State 177 which will take you south to Desert Center on I 10. The Coxcomb Mountains to your right look bleak and impassable, but had you a 4WD, you could traverse innumerable prospector's and miner's trails. As you near Desert Center, off to the right you can see Eagle Mountain; on the slopes of that mountain is a young ghost town with a high school football field with lights for night games. (The final graduation was held Memorial Day, 1983.) Eagle Mountain was a company town, owned by Kaiser Steel, and when that company moved out in 1981, the town virtually died. It is eerie to see rows of cottages with plywood over the windows and a shoppers' mall with nothing but littered vacant stores and an empty parking lot. Just before entering into Desert Center you will also find new plantations of countless acres of young jojoba plants, a bush bearing beans that will produce a miracle oil with many marvelous uses. The old wealth of the desert, a mountain of iron ore, is replaced by the new, an agricultural wonder.

Well, you are now back on I-10 and can turn the nose of your car eastward toward scenic Arizona. In your short northerly loop off the super highway, you will not have learned much intimate detail of the desert experience—the call of the canyons' curves, the tingle of danger, a wealth of flowers spilled beside a lonely road, the pavan of the stars in the cold sky seen from the warmth of your sleeping bag—but you will have at least stood briefly in the center of soul-expanding space under the big blue bowl. And if you stand in openness of mind and spirit, and if heaven is kind, it is possible that you will hear the first whisper of the lure of the desert.

*Desert flowers*

# II
# Desert Flowers

*In Butte Valley*

# 17

## You Have to Go in Convoy

*Bear ye one another's burdens, and so fulfil the law of Christ... For every man shall bear his own burden.*
*Galatians 6:2, 5*

This sermon will be a rambling explication of the Hegelian Triad. G. W. F. Hegel, a German philosopher who lived approximately from the time of the Battle of Bunker Hill to the fall of the Alamo, said that logical thought had three stages: thesis, antithesis, and synthesis. That is, you began with a truth, found an opposite truth, and put them together to get a higher, fully-orbed truth. I am throwing in the hors d'oeuvre of exposition in order that I may spread before you one of those succulent, narrative introductions which have marked my sermonic form of recent years —a long, adjective-spiced description of something that has happened to me, lavishingly written without the least need for thinking on your part or mine. Such an initial excursus is a lazy preacher's crutch. He can get a third or halfway through his sermon before it is necessary for him to buckle down to the serious work of exposition. I have set my homiletic conscience at ease in the matter of these meandering prologues because, as a true English scholar in this congregation tells me, I achieve a "unity of effect." So then, to the event from which this sermon takes its origin.

For some time a member of Messiah had been inviting me to take an off-the-road trip with him before Baja became macadamized. I had been with him on a jaunt up the old main road from La Paz (it's all hard surface now), and the roughness of the road made me decide that I didn't have the stuff to be an off-the-road driver. This time, he said enthusiastically, the jaunt would be down the long beach from San Felipe to Puertecitos, and it would have to be taken at a time of the month when low tides made the trip possible. Also, he said we would go in convoy with two other four-wheel-drive vehicles, each with skilled and experienced drivers. To be in company on the back roads in Baja is considered essential. Says one guide book:

> Side roads to remote areas . . . should be taken with caution and only with a companion vehicle. If deep soft sands are to be encountered, even four-wheel-drive vehicles should have extra wide tires. Several people traveling by themselves on side roads of Baja have broken down or become lost and found they were dangerously isolated . . . in big trouble.

But we had three four-wheel-drive cars, all well-equipped with gear and gas, and one of them with an astonishing plethora of gadgets for hauling cars out of mud and sand. So, with good, well-found rigs and experienced drivers, plus the convoy system, we seemed to be in for an easy journey over what for the ill-equipped novice would soon become a disaster area.

So after breakfast in a beach-side cafe in San Felipe (it's always fried eggs, fried potatoes, tortillas, and frijoles), we sailed merrily down the beach with the smooth Sea of Cortes—silver, cerulean, and indigo in the morning sun—to port and the baked brown aridities of the Sierra Santa Rosa towering to starboard. Out front the point car, a big V8 Jeep flying along the water's edge like the proverbial bat out of Tophet, suddenly slowed, took a cant to leeward, and stopped, hub deep on the left and hardly less so on the right. Briefly, he had hit something uncomfortably like quicksand, and after futile attempts to drive out, accompanied by much digging and scraping, both the other vehicles, hitched in series, towed him out. So we went on a bit farther and decided to strike inland. The two lead cars easily crossed a smooth flat with a white salt frosting, but the third car, a Bronco with huge tires and a heavy load, without warning, went down till the frame rested on the mud. The clay was incredibly sticky—it made foot gear on the barefoot men who helped push. No sooner was the vehicle pulled out than it plunged, twenty-five yards later, into another bog. This time, as it was being winched out, it towed the two anchor cars backward; and finally a snatch block got the bogged Bronco out onto something resembling solid ground. The beach experience need not be given in detail; one final vignette is enough. The other Bronco, unchecked till now, whistling splendidly along, hit a sharp little gully made by water running seaward from an inland salt pond and went in beyond hope of self-extrication, with the waves washing its seaward side and the tide swiftly coming in—I can close my eyes and see it now. I am afraid of salt water; all sensible boatmen are. The 7/16ths steel cable was hurriedly hitched, and for the mechanically minded, the tightness of the trap is illustrated by noting that it took the full roaring power of three engines, totalling 1000 cubic inches, delivered to twelve wheels, all in low low gear, to get that one car out.

I had been told that the next stretch, the hilly road below Puertecitos to Gonzaga Bay, was known as the "Terrible Twenty" miles because of the series of six steep grades (one of them 28 per cent) with sharp volcanic rocks—tire-killers. It lived up to its billing, and my contribution to this stretch was limited to looking at the stunning scenery and exclaiming "Wow!," not at the beauty, but at the badness of the road. I could see why there was a wayside shrine at the top of the grades. Out of necessity we turned inland at Punta Final—Last Point—and headed for a desolate place called Las Arrastras. We missed the road, got separated, and then went up a wash-type road toward Pioneer Mine; and I began to see what four-wheel-drives could do with skillful handling. At Las Arrastras we decided we had better take the "Main Road;" that is, a trail which a healthy goat could traverse with moderate ease, rather than risk the cut-off to Laguna Champalla, which all guide books describe as "very bad, even for four-wheel-drives." In part this was because there had been rain in recent days, and it was a possibility that night (all day lightning had been flickering evilly under an anvil top to the north), and it is madness to get caught in one of these washes when there is a possibility of a flash flood. But a few hundred yards out of Las Arrastras, the lead car took the wrong fork (there's never any guiding markers) and didn't hear the warning honks from behind. When the three vehicles finally gathered, and there was a general recognition we were headed for the evil fifteen miles of cutoff, it was decided to press ahead; gas was too low to go back, and two of the drivers had been through it before without even getting out of their cars.

What followed was the most unbelievable passage I have ever seen, or hope to see; and I have a strong suspicion that the experienced Baja travellers have no desire to repeat it. For we soon discovered that a day or two before a flash flood had ripped out sections of the bad road and left nothing but a boulder-strewn stream bed. As darkness was coming down, after travelling what would be considered by rational men an impassable stretch, we came to the first really bad place. I walked ahead and returned convinced that it was utterly impossible to get through. Undaunted, the veterans cheerfully tackled the passage. The first car was the big Jeep; it took forty-five minutes to get it moved the first fifteen feet. The Jeep pickup was wide and long; in one place there was an inch to spare on one side and about two inches on the other; the rocky canyon was that tight a fit. There was no turning around. But the narrower Broncos lurched through faster, and the next stage of road building was undertaken.

Boulders were rolled to fill holes and to make ramps over giants too big to be moved. We had one Herculean youth whose talents were abundantly employed in this toil. As those of you who have gone to Retreat know, I like to lug rocks to make dams. But I was out of my class here; I had to stand aside for better men; I felt old. About nine o'clock our Messiah man came by with a squirming rattlesnake held tightly behind the head, and a rest was indicated. Refreshed, the stout hearts and stalwart muscles went to road building again. I give no more details. It's enough to say that less than two miles, with about 400 yards that were really bad, took almost six hours to do. We entered that boulder-cursed and snake-haunted defile in daylight; we came to the star-blessed top of the pass at midnight. The rocks had modified the corners of all the cars. It had been hard work physically; there was the emotional strain of the possibility of rain (fortunately it didn't come); there was always a chance that something mechanical would break under the outrageous battering; and hence the joy of victory was unrefined. A great cheering fire was kindled, but it was too much work for weary men to cook, so the caloric deficiences of the group (save for one virtuous teetotaler) were remedied by quantities of excellent Mexican rum in Schweppes Bitter Lemon. Sensibly, three of us crawled into our sleeping bags a little after one and were only drowsily aware of the songs and recitations that polluted the cool night air until the hint of dawn was in the east.

Well, more might be said, but it is time to point the moral and adorn the tale. The lesson is that the journey could not have been by any *one* vehicle or *one* driver, though the machines were designed for rough going and the drivers were experienced. Only the convoy system made the trip possible. The group got through where the solitary traveller could not have survived; and this is a parable of man's journey through the desert of time and sense we call this world. As in the treacherous sands and stony gorges of Baja, so in the pilgrimage of life, the lone traveler walks in greater hazard than he who has capable and concerned companions. Occasionally a solitary pilgrim makes it by rare luck and toughness, but for the majority of men and women in their trek through time, fellowship and help are necessities. You have to go in convoy.

Let's look at our text and note the paradox which Paul sets before us; it's an intriguing contradiction. Mark the second verse of Galatians: "Bear ye one another's burdens, and so fulfil the law of Christ." That's the Christian statement of the principle of altruism—the brotherhood of man. We're put in this world to help each other. But Paul's second text is curiously at variance with his first word: "For every man shall bear his own burden." This is more like the philsophy Jeremy Bentham, that strange English genius, put forth—enlightened self-interest. How reconcile it with the concern for others which marks our first text? I spoke earlier of the Hegelian Triad: thesis, antithesis, and higher synthesis—the truth, its opposite, and the full-orbed combination of the two. Paul is seldom simplistic, and in his treatment of human relationship at this point, he is provocatively complex. Now if we take the Sunday-School-type first text—that we are to think of others, bear the burdens of others—we do get something fine and likable. Unselfish people are the salt of the earth; the men and women who have a deep concern for those in trouble show a shining side of the Christian life. Messiah has exhibited this trait in its giving to missions. Although we are but a small Church, about $17,000 passed through our books last year to help others. Some of it we generated; some of it we only channeled; but to help the financially less fortunate bear their burdens has been a characteristic of our Church, and one that we ought never to neglect. In a world of selfishness, where most men are looking out for number one, where the weak and the poor suffer in silent neglect, the candle of concern shines golden in the darkness. This we believe and often practice. The point doesn't need much development. It's the thesis of our theme today.

But what of Paul's second text—"For every man shall bear his own burden"? How is it to be reconciled with altruism? First let it be noted that self-sufficiency is a virtue, though less hailed from pulpits than care for others. For one thing, only those with good egos can make much of Christ's doctrine to love your neighbor as yourself, for if you love yourself little, small will be your love for your neighbors. Again, self-reliance is a necessary quality for a full life. I well remember the thrill I got as a young man in reading Ralph Waldo Emerson's famous essay, "Self-Reliance." "Trust thyself," says the key sentence, "every fiber must vibrate to that iron string." People who have no confidence in themselves are less than whole; people who cannot carry their own burdens, at least in part and for some of the time, are unfruitful vines in the garden of humanity. The admonition to bear your own burdens, therefore, is not merely an exhortation to selfishness; it is advice of broad social usefulness. The individual's relationship to society should not be parasitic. He should not expect to be carried on the backs of the toilers; the world doesn't owe him a living at all. Handicapped, yes; disadvantaged, yes; but simply lazy and spineless, no. And sad as it is to consider, there is a human tendency for people to become parasitic if they are certain that somebody else is going to bear their economic burdens. A true relation of the individual and society is symbiotic, not parasitic. In a parasite-host relationship the one lives wholly at the expense of the other; in a symbiosis, each part of the union does something for the other. A good marriage certainly blends Paul's two principles; husband and wife do bear each other's burdens; and at the same time each partner personally carries a share of the load. The old concept of man and woman as oak and clinging vine was silly long before women's lib came along. In our roles as Church members we must do our share for the Church, and yet have our burdens borne in part by those who are bound to us in agape. The best friendships are those in which each friend is willing to carry his share of the load, and at the same time be ready to accept help from the other when his own strength fails.

Let me return to our convoy symbol. It was well that the three vehicles went together through treacherous sand and dark rocky canyons, but it should not be forgotten that each one of these three was a strong, well-designed conveyance; each could contribute to the symbiosis the convoy was. This thesis of helpfulness and its antithesis of self-sufficiency forms the higher synthesis of a good relationship among men.

Almost parenthetically I draw your attention to the way in which one aspect of the total truth is overstressed in our time. Literature, the movies (the pictures of the late Jean Renoir are examples), and the tube tend to feature the loner, the solitary proud man who meets life without help. He is fiercely independent, or perhaps not fierce, but still independent. Roger Miller's song, "King of the Road"—the man without family, money, permanent lodging,or even cigarettes—is a lyrical example to the totally self-reliant aspect of living, the man who doesn't drive in convoy. And we know these people well: the souls who dwell apart; the withdrawn, the proud, they who profess to need no love or nearness. This I say of them, that usually the loner is a loser. Life is too much for the strongest, and there come times when the mud and rocks and steep climbs are too much for the toughest to conquer unaided. Be self-reliant; be self-reliant—but don't be too self-reliant.

Let me concludingly add another dimension to the concept of convoy —the divine dimension. For there come times in life when human help is not enough. When the man went down from Jerusalem to Jericho in the desert country east of the holy city on a lonely, robber-haunted road of heat and harshness, he needed human help when he fell among the thieves; the good Samaritan staunched his wound, put him on his own beast, and they went in small convoy to the inn. This was human concern and help at its simple best. But sometimes more is needed. Paul, a few verses earlier in Galatians, points to the necessary More. "If we live in the Spirit," he tells us, "let us also walk in the Spirit." Long centuries ago the children of Israel came out of Egypt, and long they wandered in the cruel desert of the Sinai peninsula. They were banded together for help—all twelve tribes—but they had a greater than human Guide. In the vast hot wilderness God was with them. "In the daytime He led them with a cloud, and all the night with a light of fire." We read also in the Scriptures that after the crucifixion two disciples were going along the road to Emmaus when dusk was coming down; they walked with sad hearts and talked with sorrow. "And it came to pass that Jesus Himself drew near and went with them." Thus the Divine Man walked with the lesser men, and this Holy Companionship is yours for the asking. Blessed and safe are you in your early pilgrimage when you have made yourself strong, journey in a company of the concerned, and have God Himself as your Guide and Guardian.

—*Congregational Church of the Messiah, 1974.*

## 18

## The Unconquest of Black Mountain

> And when Jesus was come into his own country, he taught them in their synagogue . . . And he did not many mighty works there.
> *Matthew 13:54, 58*

This is a sermon about not making it, about failing to win. It deals with an inescapable fact of the human condition—that we are going to lose some battles we really want to win; that we are going to be defeated at a point where victory would be of great significance; that there are some jobs we can't get, some rivers we can't cross, some mountains we can't climb. This is a hard fact to face, not only because of our inherent hunger to get the thing we greatly desire, but also because we live in a success-oriented culture, and the man or woman who doesn't win must not only know loss, but the sting of scorn or pity. In more open and manifest competitions men face, the competitor is lashed on by such sayings as Red Sander's aphorism: "Winning isn't the most important thing; it's the only thing." In the entertainment world there is a savage behind-the-scenes fight for spots and billings. Fame, for male or female, is a scarce commodity; and the small supply is fiercely fought for by many. This much is pretty obvious; what I want to talk with you about today is something a bit subtler, but nontheless common—the failure to reach an attainable goal we have set for ourselves and work for in the hope of attainment. When we realize that we aren't going to make it, how should we react? How can we best cope with the inevitable defeats of life?

By way of background for our expository thinking, let me tell, as has been my wont in recent years, a personal parable. Five years ago (lacking precisely a week) Mrs. Butman and I walked away from an accident in

Tucumcari, New Mexico, which totaled our car, but left us virtually unscathed. We had no right to be alive after that wreck, and I decided to take warning by it. I resolved that often—once a week if possible—I would take a day off (up till then I ran pretty much to a seven-day week) and go out into the open spaces and enjoy such time as was left to me. In this way I became acquainted with the El Paso Mountains, about which I have told no few yarns. I went through the three major canyons—Iron, Mesquite, and Last Chance—on foot, and explored many of the byways, finding dazzling rock formations and a lone spring with a mountain lion's pawprint in the mud, and such like delights. But one place I never got to —Black Mountain, highest peak of the El Pasos, a treeless summit that pushes into the blue desert sky about ten miles north of where the back road to Death Valley leaves Route 14 at Red Rock Canyon, where, incidentally and sadly, a young girl met death on the highway when a flash flood roared across the main road and swept her away.

Black Mountain fascinated me. I was told by the one filling station owner near it, that there was an Indian graveyard on the summit; and people living in the canyons said that it could be climbed, although there were no trails to the top. Knowing that I was going to Cornwall to walk the cliffs, I resolved to get into hiking condition. I lost weight, did exercises, trudged faithfully back and forth to and from the Church, and hardened my legs in a number of training hikes. One of them got me to a minor knoll part way up Black Mountain, and I felt that given a long day I could make it all the way. So on a cool morning in spring off I went with high hopes that by sundown my dream of nearly five years' standing would be actualized. I drove my abused Monte Carlo (Captain Silver has no business in those canyons) to a spot where Mesquite Canyon road becomes a four-wheel-drive trail.

A mile-and-a-half walk brought me to the place where the ascent was to begin. With lightly loaded leather rucksack on my back and rubber-tipped walking stick in hand, I started up. Soon I reached the knoll that was my previous ultima Thule. I looked over the terrain and decided that instead of walking along a ridge, I would cut across; and so I set out confidantly on a 45 degree slope that dropped off into a secondary canyon five hundred feet down. In five minutes I began to worry; the shale was loose; it slid, and my feet slipped. In ten minutes I had to hang onto shrubs that were not really strong enough to hang on to; I was drenched with sweat. In fifteen minutes I was seriously concerned if I was going to get to solid rock again. I did, just barely, heart pounding and legs aching. On hard ledge once more, I looked back at the little distance I had come, and up and up at the steep heights yet to go—a passage far longer and harder than that which I had precariously traversed. I knew at that moment that I wasn't going to make it to Black Mountain's top, that day, or ever.

So I turned back, carefully picking my way down the treacherous slope to the dry gulch far below. The going was tough enough to keep me from doing more than wonder how I was going to get safely to the sand at the bottom of the wash. But when I got to the easy going, awareness of defeat began to well up. I am a competitor; generally if I want to do something physical, I can do it. Of course I realize that the speed and strength and toughness of youth are long gone, but still I can usually accomplish what I set out to do. Not this time. Black Mountain was there; and it would never be conquered by me. I took off my pack, sat down and brooded on the bitterness of being beaten. Then I opened my pack, took out the little flask of wine I had hoped to quaff in triumph up on the summit with nothing above me but the clean desert sky, and stood up to toast the victor: "Black Mountain," I said, "you're a better man than I am."

Upon the thin thread of this narrative, let me string a few pearls of thought—beads of varying worth. First of all, be it noted that it is important to have a goal, even though that goal is not rare or great. A scoffer could reasonably say to me, "You didn't make it to the top of Black Mountain. So what? What's so wonderful about climbing that obscure peak hardly a mile high? It's been done countless times, and there are probably many durable ancients, older than yourself, who could have reached the top without working up a sweat. Even if you had done it, what really would you have accomplished?"

To which I make answer: the goalless life is a drab and sterile life. A person is not really living unless he has something to strive for, however insignificant that object may be in the eyes of others. The nature or rarity of the goal, in a sense, is unimportant; the importance lies in the desire that makes you suffer and strive and toil. Perhaps you may want a certain picture or piece of furniture, or to cultivate a rare plant (it doesn't have to be the white marigold). You want to step up at work, to gain the friendship or love of a desirable person, to lose weight, to get good marks, to be able to pray better, to have a good vacation. I'm deliberately leaving out any ascending order of values in this random list, so as to stress the necessity of a goal, any goal (I almost dare say, even a bad goal). Sir Edmund Hillary and Torgay Tensing have made it to the top of Everest, ridgepole of the world, but such an Homeric achievement, and its like, are beyond the reach of all but the strong and lucky. I heard this point of the need for a goal stretched out into an after-dinner address this summer, when at the National Association Annual Meeting, Robert Gadbury spoke on the topic, "Everyday Everests." It was a meaty thought. The Himalayas aren't available to us, and even if they were, we lack the strength and skill and resources to scale them. But to have a minor mountain peak, near at hand, within the possibility of conquest, is of the essence for rich exciting living, be that goal a new car, a better house, or the conquest of a besetting, deadly sin.

But let's screw the focus a little finer. What of the available Everest that you ought to be able to climb—and can't? Here is a second lesson from the unconquest of Black Mountain. That hill was available—two hours and a half away in miles and time, not a thing of great peril nor filled with sheer facades calling for crampons and pitons and climbing axes and a team of skilled and dedicated mountaineers. It was an ordinary mountain, and I couldn't make it, just as many of you haven't been able to reach the reachable low goals you have set for yourself. There are desirable objects almost within reach, but you just can't stretch quite far enough. Further, there is the galling fact that we sometimes fail when we have taken our best shot. I had worked hard to get in shape; behind my abortive attempt lay many years of general physical discipline, and a year of specific effort for that particular climb. There are things that you ought to be able to do, jobs that you should be able to get, attitudes you should be able to overcome—and you have failed despite your best efforts. You don't have the excuse that you weren't trying, or you didn't know how, or that the grapes were sour anyhow. No, you wanted to climb your Black Mountain, you wanted to stand on the summit of your local available Everest, and you had to turn back, beaten.

Well, as you sip the bitter tea of failure, take comfort in this: You're in good company. There are many mighty men and women, geniuses, the rich and powerful, kings and queens, who have had to face failure in something they set out to do. But instead of calling a roll of these illustrious peak scalers who couldn't make their Black Mountain, I ask you to look at Jesus himself, who knew exactly this sort of failure. Did you listen carefully to the Scripture reading? Jesus didn't make it in Nazareth, his home town. Our text, taken from Matthew, simply says that he could do few mighty works in his own country because of their unbelief. Luke is far more graphic. The congregation in his own house of worship, where he had been trained in faith as a boy, dragged him out to a cliff at the edge of town to throw him off and kill him. Jesus generalized almost philosophically: "A prophet is not without honor, save in his own country and in his own house." But we do his human nature less than justice if we suppose that this rejection by his own did not rankle and burn. Jesus Christ, scaler of such Everests of the spirit as no other man has ever conquered, failed at home. The conquest of his home town, the scrubby little village of Nazareth, was beyond him. He shares with us, and we share with him, the ache of defeat where we wanted to win, and where winning was a possibility.

What are we to do when we find that we can't climb our Black Mountain? What reactions are possible? It is not the brutal and inevitable fact of defeat that is ultimately important (for this comes to all), but how we react to it. For we can find victory in defeat and defeat in defeat, and I am not being redundant in this latter: outward defeat is of the moment; interior defeat etches itself irradicably upon the soul; it saps spiritual stamina; it rots character. Now, while there is a certain adrenalin-producing value in the coach's exhortation, "A team that won't be beat can't be beat," in a very real sense this is foolish. Any team can be beaten, and eventually all teams are beaten; and so it is with the single soul facing life's foes. So then, what can we do with the fact of defeat? Well, we can take the crybaby response—the referees are crooked; the ball didn't bounce right; our pet play wasn't called. We can sit and sulk over the unfairness of fate in denying us our wish in the thing we wanted so much and tried so hard to get. Or we can deny defeat, say that it didn't happen, shut our eyes to the clear event, delude ourselves that we could have done it if we really wanted to; or that tomorrow, or next week, or next month, or sometime, we will do it.

My advice is to accept defeat, but accept it in a creative way. Simple acceptance is not quite enough. I have always liked Thomas Carlyle's acid put-down of ebullient Margaret Fuller, the transcendentalist poet of yesterday's New England. Cried Margaret, "I accept the universe." Growled Thomas, "Gad, she'd better." There's such a thing as accepting defeat too gracefully; we give in too easily, and cease to stretch the muscles of heart and mind and soul. But when we have done our best and yet have failed, we must learn and practice the high art of snatching victory from the jaws of apparent defeat. This is not rhetoric; it is the simple truth. Dull is he who does not learn from his lickings; unhappy is she who does not inwardly meet the blows of harsh exterior reality. I briefly suggest two ways of turning failure to account: one is to realize that life is not a thing of the flesh alone, but of the Spirit; the other—and greater—is to realize that life is best when God rules it.

I illustrate the first truth in a tangential way. We must all come to a place where we realize that our physical powers are not what they once were; the sheer exuberant zest of life, the mere living, inexorably dwindles and fades. But we need not suppose that the joy of life is dependent simply on muscle tone. We are not beasts, whose delights are of the flesh alone; we are men and women with souls.

One day in May I was walking along the cliffs of Cornwall between Mousehole and Lamorna, delighting in the flowers that grew in rich purple abundance on that well-watered slope, yet sorrowing that my legs were not going to be able to carry me as far as I wanted to go. As I paused to rest, a man approached me from the other direction, a small man, but wiry, and with that indefinable air that marks the Englishmen of breeding. We fell into conversation, and he told me that the purple blooms I admired had the homely name of Ragged Robin, and added that it had been his custom for many years (he was about my age, I should judge) to come down from Gloucestershire to walk the coastal path. When I lamented that I had long wanted to make this jaunt, but found that I could no longer do as much of it as swiftly as I once could, he made a wise comment. "Ah," he said, "I know it. But now we can take it at our own pace." I knew what he meant: with time's defeat of sinew and lungs, came a wisdom time could not touch. We didn't have to break records; we didn't have to crowd ourselves to make the number of miles we had set for ourselves in the morning. Freed from these compulsions, we could savor the sea and the smells, sip with appreciation the wine of the beauty all about us; no longer hurried, no longer under the savage imperatives of distance to be run or time to be made. When you can't make it to the top of life's Black Mountain, when you can't get what you want, you are free to enjoy and absorb the beauty and reality that are within reach.

And we can do this best when we truly realize that our lives are God's and He alone is the arbiter of triumph or defeat. I dislike saying that God has a plan for each life, for it seems to be a trite and prosy word; yet its ineluctable truth forces me to say it. It's one thing to be beaten by life at some point where you wanted victory with a wanting nearly erotic in its intensity. It's something else, and better, to realize that if you are set in the will of God, whatever happens—even the exhausted stop on the slope of your Black Mountain—is His intent for you. And out of this realization grows the faith that there is a life beyond in which we will scale peaks far higher than those petty eminences that baffled us in this world of time and sense. The only summit Christ knew at Nazareth was the clifftop his townsmen would have cast him from; but he went on to climb the greater Black Mountain of Calvary, and at the last to put all things under his feet.
—*Congregational Church of the Messiah, 1975.*

## 19

## The Beautiful and Friendly Beasts

Say to the Daughter of Zion
Look, your King comes to you;
He is humble, he rides on a donkey
And on a colt, the foal of a beast of burden.
*Matthew 21:5 (J.B.)*

Who gave the wild donkey his freedom.
And untied the rope from his proud neck?
I have given him the desert as a home,
The salt plains as his own habitat.
*Job 39:11, 12 (J.B.)*

Since this sermon will be formless and rhapsodic, I think it well to say at the start that it does have a definite theme. Christmas is a time when we try to have good relationships with our fellow men, and, to a degree, less stressed with God. We reach out and up in seeking for good will toward man, and in glorifying God. I suggest that we add a third dimension to the spiritual reach by showing kindness to, and appreciation for, the beasts who are below us in intelligence and privileges. Blessed be High God and fellow humans, and the beautiful and friendly beasts. This is the thrust of our thinking today.

    This sermon roots in a rare and splendid sight I saw two weeks ago in the Saline Valley. Early on the day after Thanksgiving my son and I fared northward in my little high-visibility orange Datsun truck. Aided by a strong south wind, we went swiftly by the familiar El Paso Mountains, past Searles Dry Lake and the huge chemical plants of Westend and Trona. We lunched at the top of the pass overlooking desolate Panamint Valley, and hurried on, leaving to starboard the austere Panamint

Range, with its canyons—Sunrise, Pleasant, Happy—and tall Telescope Peak, sentinel to Death Valley—that romantically named, but now highly-publicized and somewhat crowded bowl. We were going to a less inhabited place—Saline Valley, the loneliest plain in Southern California. We headed west for a while on Route 190, passing Panamint Springs and Father Crowley's Memorial, and then turned north through the Santa Rosa Hills. The map was a trifle ambiguous, and the dirt road, while newly graded, seemed endless, and we wondered if we had lost our way. But finally, at a point with a superb view of northern Panamint Valley and the Cottonwood Range, we plunged and lurched down switchbacks of Grapevine Canyon. A snowstorm was darkly brooding over the Nelson Range to port, and its purple gloom made the great white flats of Saline Valley stand out in stark chalky relief. The valley was lonesome enough, with but one permanent house in its eighty-seven-mile length of dirt road, but on this weekend there were many four-wheel-drive vehicles coming down from the north.

We pushed on, but darkness was descending, and as we began to climb out of the northern end of the valley into the Inyo Mountains, the road worsened, the cold and wind strengthened, and we could see another snowstorm ahead, so we turned back to make camp in a sheltered spot near Willow Creek. As we went, we saw some blurred forms of animals near the base of the cliffs—burros, I judged them to be. We dined and drank and were comfortable by lantern light as night settled down, cloudy and cold. One foolish young couple in a four-wheel-drive, seeing the cheery light of our lantern in the lonely gloom, came seeking help. They were totally lost and had no map. We directed them back to Darwin Falls and wished them well in climbing the Grapevine Canyon grade.

The morning was stimulating, icy, and finger-numbing, with the sun coming over the eastern mountains to touch the peaks of the Inyos, first with red and pink, and then gold. Only a few miles out of Willow Creek we saw a superlative sight—the burros we had seen the night before. But these were misnamed, for they were large and splendid with shiny black and gray fur, proud, alert, fearless. This family numbered four—the big male, the mother only slightly smaller, and two leggy colts. They were near and clear, and our eyes rejoiced and our hearts exulted at the sight of them: glossy black, lustrous gray, jewels of life set in a vast frame of treeless tan and ocher mountains, pale dunes, and white lake bed, grand beyond words under the arching naked sky and the great gold eye of the sun. Now I had a mental stereotype of the mule, the jackass, the donkey, as mean and mangy creatures, but these beasts of the wild were glorious in their pride and freedom. Watching, I understood for the first time what the writer of the Book of Job meant when he makes God challenge Job with the stunning fact of the wild ass. Cries the Creator:

> Who gave the wild donkey his freedom
> And untied the rope from his proud neck?
> I have given him the desert as a home,
> The salt plains as his own habitat.
> He scorns the turmoil of the town;
> There are no shouts from a driver for him to listen for.
> The mountains are the pastures that he ranges
> In quest of any type of green blade or leaf.

And with this astonishingly apposite pean from a point of Asia, we leave this (is it sacrilegious to say holy?) family, free and proud in its remote pasture.

I think perhaps that I should now come down to earth and give you a little fact-laden prose by way of change of literary pace. I have long intended to get the nomenclature of the ass family straightened out in my own mind, and having to speak to precisionists like the Messiah congregation is an occasion to do so, so I will now give you a short essay on the ass, or donkey, for the terms are synonymous. The name comes from the Latin *asinus*, a loan word from Asia Minor, and it applies to any of the several quadrupeds of the genus *equus*, all smaller than the horse, with shorter mane, shorter hair on the tail, and long ears. The domestic ass, *equus asininus*, is patient, slow, sure-footed, and a symbol of obstinancy and stupidity. The wild ass, of which Job tells, is found in Asia and North Africa and is gregarious, wary, and fleet-footed. Technically, the wild ass is a kiang, a large dark beast. The onager is like, but smaller and paler. Now when we speak of the common mule, we are talking about a rather intricate creature. A mule is generally the offspring of a male ass and a female horse. The mule has long ears, large head, small hooves, with the form and size of a horse. Mules are very strong with great endurance and sure-footedness. They are highly intelligent, and Robert Heinlein, in one of his science fiction novels, tells with affection of Buck, the wise, talking mule, man's advisor in a pioneer situation on some nameless planet. The male mule is called a jackass or a donkey, but we should take note of the hinny, which is a hybrid between a stallion and a she-ass. Mules are generally sterile—the penalty nature exacts for cross-breeding—but hinnys sometime foal. The hinny differs from the mule, which is proverbially mean, being gentle in disposition. A burro is a small donkey, a burden bearer; and a jenny is a female donkey.

This lecture delivered, let's look now at the donkey as this beast is seen in song, poetry, and Holy Writ, together with some random explications. The splendid animal of which the Book of Job tells, and which enthralled us in the lonely valley, was a wild ass; and wildness is an essential element for all life, tamed and urban man particularly. In his essay, "Higher Laws," Thoreau opens by saying:

> As I came home through the woods . . . I caught a glimpse of a woodchuck stealing across my path . . . and was strongly tempted to seize and devour him raw: not that I was hungry then, except for that wildness which he represented . . . I found in myself, and still find, an instinct toward a higher, or as it is named, spiritual life, as do most men, and another toward a primitive rank and savage one, and I reverence them both. I love the wild not less than the good.

There is in our time a great push for the outdoors; it is an escape from the enmassment and strangulation of our increasingly regimented city life. I am less crowded than most men, I suppose, and yet something in me would die if I could not regularly get out into the empty places—the canyons, the ridges, and the deserts—all lonely and free of people (at the time at least). They touch an ancient chord of wildness in me which will not cease to resonate. Wildness is linked to the need to be free, and the hunger for freedom is an essential and enduring part of the human psyche; it outlasts civilizations. I wrote, some twenty years ago, a sermon on this theme, "Coyote on La Brea," which dealt with that desert ranger as strangely seen in the heart of a great metropolis. And I echo the ending of that sermon by saying that it may well be that ten thousand years from now, when Los Angeles is one with Nineveh and Tyre, the coyotes, the burros, the wild horses, the wolves, and the mountain lions will again roam this big basin, once the city of a civilization greater than that of Ozymandias or the mighty Persian monarch Jamshyd, of whom Omar Khayyam sang, as he hymned the free beast we praise this morning:

> They say the lion and the lizard keep
> The courts where Jamshyd gloried and drank deep,
> And Bahram, the great hunter, the wild ass,
> Stamps o'er his head, but cannot break his sleep.

But we need not turn to pagan poetry to find the donkey praised. I cite but two instances, both dealing with the ass as that beast took part in the story of Christ. G. K. Chesterton sings wry tribute in his poem, "The Donkey":

> When fishes flew and forests walked
>     And figs grew upon thorn,
> Some moment when the moon was blood
>     Then surely I was born:
>
> With monstrous head and sickening cry
>     And ears like errant wings,
> The devil's walking parody
>     On all four-footed things;
>
> The tattered outlaw of the earth
>     Of ancient crooked will:
> Starve, scourge me, deride me: I am dumb,
>     I keep my secret still.
>
> Fools! For I also have my hour;
>     One far fierce hour and sweet:
> There was a shout about my ears,
>     And palms before my feet.

On the day of the triumphal entry into Jerusalem, Christ rode, not upon the war horse, the charger, mount of the bloody warlord, the mighty stallion, but on a colt, the foal of a donkey.

> Say to the daughter of Zion
> Look, your King comes to you;
> He is humble, he rides on a donkey
> And on a colt, the foal of a beast of burden.

And it is one of the sweet parts of the Christmas story that the little Lord Jesus was born in a manger, in a stable with the cattle lowing, surrounded by friendly beasts. There is a carol which tells of the burro's part in Christ's birth:

> Jesus, our brother, kind and good
> Was humbly born in a manger rude,
> And the friendly beasts around him stood:
> Jesus, our brother, kind and good.
>
> "I," said the donkey, shaggy and brown,
> "I carried his mother up hill and down,
> I carried her safely to Bethlehem town,
> I," said the donkey, shaggy and brown.

There is a legend, to be found in the folklore of many countries, that the animals, as a reward for their Bethlehem vigil over the Mother and Child, were given the power to speak on Christmas Eve. And here I cannot resist repeating a story told to me long ago by Father Felix Bartrop, an Episcopal priest who, like myself, was a lover of things strange and inexplicable. He said that as a young curate he was assigned to a country parish near Portsmouth, New Hampshire. The day before Christmas he happened to visit a farmer parishioner, a Pole or Bohemian, I cannot remember which, and found the man in his barn, deeply disturbed because a prize heifer was very sick. The farmer appeared at early mass on Christmas morning, and Father Bartrop asked about the sick creature.

"She died sometime last night," said the farmer.

Something in his tone caught the cleric's attention.

"Don't you know when?" he asked. "Didn't you stay with her?"

The farmer looked at him.

"Do you think I would go into a barn on Christmas Eve?" he asked.

He was a prudent man. He would not risk the panic fear of hearing dumb creatures speak at midnight.

I have said that we might well, in the Advent and Christmas season, show mercy and kindness to animals, for it is written in the Word: "A merciful man is merciful to his beast." The animal demands of us its spiritual right, the quality of mercy. Yet just how to show this is no easy matter. It's a complex business, as the continuing quarrel between the conservationist and the hunter witnesses. The conservationist, sometimes in such wildly unfair accusations as the TV show, "The Guns of Autumn," sees the hunter as the cruel witless predator killing the harmless deer. The counter to that view may be seen in Rick O'Shay's and Hipshot's and Qyatt's idyllic elk hunts as winter begins. Now I confess that I have no longer a love for hunting, and yet I am aware of the sense of the hunter's report, which many game wardens chorus, that "harvesting" deer when an area is overpopulated is kinder than the slow death by starvation that comes to many yearlings when the snows are deep and the forage scarce. But this complexity stated, I was disturbed by an article in the *Los Angeles Times* which came hard on the heels of my sight of the gorgeous wild things of Saline Valley. I was shocked to read this item, which I quote in its terse entirety.

> Wild burros in the California desert are eating other animals out of their natural habitat, the National Advisory Board on Wild Free Roaming Horses and Burros was told by scientists and conservation group representatives at a public hearing in Ridgecrest. They asked for immediate action to reduce the number of burros said to be overgrazing sparse desert vegetation and destroying irreplaceable water-

shed used by desert bighorn sheep, desert tortoises, and rodents. There are an estimated 3500 wild burros scattered over 25 million acres of California Desert.

I think that I am too prejudiced by my morning vision of the four-footed family of desert dwellers to react coolly to this proposal. "Immediate action to reduce the number" is, of course, an euphemism for shooting them, the final solution to the burro problem, as it were. And I can visualize all too clearly these beautiful and friendly beasts, harming no man, enduring the icy cold and furnace heat of that dry and lonesome valley, wresting their meager meals from the barren hillside and salt flats, coming close to a car some fatal morning, as they have done many times in the past without harm, eyes bright, ears pricked up, pelts shiny in the sun, curiously and fearlessly gazing at the vehicle of death, not knowing that in seconds hot lead would hurtle from blazing rifles to drop them, limp and torn on the harsh earth they had freely roamed. I have become weary of man's tampering with ecosystems in the sacred name of ecology. Let the better beasts live, whichever they may be.

*Burros in Butte Valley*

If we have a true reverence for life, we will have it for animals as well as for humans. We share this globe with creatures less in power than we. Many of them are harmless, and ask only to be left alone; and we should not only be concerned about the beasts of the wild, but about the domestic pets that add grace and joy to our lives. I do not understand how people can take unwanted pets to strange places and heartlessly abandon them. When we consider the exuberant affection of gamboling dogs, their questioning looks, and the grace, charm, and dignity of cats, and think of how animals shape themselves after the people with whom they live, their endearing habits, and the place they make for themselves in the lives of those who care for them, we see this cruelty to animals as wickedness of a very evil sort.

I am convinced that animals have rudimentary souls, the seeds of mature souls. They have a sense of ethics, loyalty, personality. I think they can do something like worship us, who are the only gods within their ken. I do not think that I am drawing long bow of imagination or analogy when I say that our Abyssinian cat, Robbie, has something that I call a devotional habit. Sometimes, at two or three o'clock in the morning, when no one has spoken to him or touched him, he will begin to purr loudly in the silence of the bedroom for no apparent reason. And I frankly call this a hymn of praise and thanksgiving. He is rejoicing in warmth and love and life, and saying his gratitude in the only language he has.

This sermon, I said initially, was a rhapsody, and perhaps I am getting a bit too rhapsodic, but if Saint Francis loved all manner of beasts, even the great wolf that terrorized the city, but licked the saint's hand when Francis preached the Gospel to him, I suppose that I have some basis in hagiography for my excess of speaking, and I also suppose that bird lovers could justly chide me for neglecting our feathered friends. But I say in ending, that in this season of the year when we cherish good will toward men and glorify God, our Giving Father, we might well remember Him who was born among beasts, who spoke of the sparrow and the eagle, the foxes in their holes, the sheep scattered on the hillside, the ox caught in a pit; and who taught us the law of love. Surely He would approve of our mercy and kindness toward those beautiful and friendly beasts who share this planet earth with us.

—*Congregational Church of the Messiah, 1975.*

# 20

# The Three Dust Devils at Coyote Dry Lake

> ... a dry land, and a wilderness, a land wherein no man dwelleth.
> *Jeremiah 51:43*
>
> ... a great and strong wind rent the mountains, and brake in pieces the rocks before the Lord: but the Lord was not in the wind.
> *I Kings 19:11*
>
> Ho, every one that thirsteth, come ye to the waters.
> *Isaiah 55:1*

This will be a rather off-beat communion homily, yet it is not without scriptural basis and spiritual content. The basic thought came to me as I sat, about a week ago, on a spur on the northern edge of the Calico Mountains, and looked out over desolate Coyote Dry Lake north of Barstow on the way to Fort Irwin. As I sat there in the solitary worship which is my custom when I am not near a Church, my mind went back to a sight I had seen the day before. And I preface the observation with a few words of background. I had driven out to Fort Irwin on Friday and, courtesy of George Vogel, had been billeted in the Bachelor Officer's Quarters. At sundown Friday the fierce north wind that smote all the southland began to rage. White dust swirled through the cantonment, the trees writhed under the savage blasts, the dormitory shook with the impact. I was glad I was under cover warmer and more substantial than canvas or camper shell. The fury subsided a bit the next day, but the wind was still high as I set out to explore the Mojave just south of the fort. I turned up a nameless road of uncertain termination since it ran into the naval gunnery range east and south of Randsburg, but it was a good road, as such roads go, and I followed it a dozen miles or so and then parked. I decided to walk to a distant ridge and before I had gone a mile my truck disappeared as even bright colored objects have a way of doing on the flat and seemingly barren desert. I reached a point half way up the ridge and sat down. The scene was stunning. The air was clean and cold, the basin was empty of all signs of human habitation or mark; even the road had disappeared in the carpet of chaparral. The valley below me was as it had been during this geological era: empty, austerely beautiful. And as I sat there, at one with the wilderness, I thought of a sight I had seen as I had come up the road some five miles back. I had stopped to study the map but my eye was taken by a strange spectacle on Coyote Dry Lake, some twenty miles away. Three towering white dust devils almost precisely the same height, and equidistant, stood in a strange pattern. I have often seen dust devils, as I am sure most of you have, but never three of such size, equality of height, and precision of spacing. Even at this distance, their whirl was visible, and they spun in the still strong wind, marching in an eerie choreography. When I came back in the afternoon they were gone, but their after-image was sharply printed in color on my mind's eye.

*Sand storm over Death Valley dunes*

And it was on this interior vision that I brooded as a part of my silent worship on the Sabbath morning. What meaning could be found in that ghostly trinity of immense vortices? I saw them as three symbols of anti-life: aridity, turbulence, and impermanence. The dust devil is found only when the land is dry and thirsty; it can rise only when the violence of powerful winds or thermal eddies swirl it aloft; its life is brief, and with the dying of the wind these tall specters collapse into the dust of the desert. In this trio of whirlings I saw symbols of the ill state of life in our time.

It is a dry and sterile day we live in, as T. S. Eliot said over half a century ago, in that important but exceedingly cryptic poem, "The Waste Land." He caught, as Louis Utermeyer tells us, "the image of an arid world" and "its sense of sterility." Certain of the poem's lines catch the terror of the desert:

> A heap of broken images, where the sun beats,
> And the dead tree gives no shelter, the cricket no relief,
> And the dry stone no sound of water. Only
> There is shadow under this red rock,
> (Come in under the shadow of this red rock),
> And I will show you something different from either
> Your shadow at morning striding behind you
> Or your shadow at evening rising to meet you;
> I will show you fear in a handful of dust.

In "The Hollow Men" Eliot speaks of

> Our dried voices, when
> We whisper together
> Are quiet and meaningless
> As wind in dry grass
> Or rats' feet over broken glass
> In our dry cellar.

Such is life in the world that ends "not with a bang, but a whimper"—a civilization which "has lost spiritual significance and has devoted itself to material standards and mechanical escapes" of this civilization.

> ...The wind shall say: here were the decent godless people:
> Their only monument the asphalt road
> And a thousand lost golf balls.

So much for aridity out of which the social dust devils spring. But they do so only because of the enormous turbulence of the winds of change that blow in our years. Ours is a broken day, a time of troubles, and old stabilities are shaken. The ancient landmarks are cast down, the regimes have given place to things new and strange. Here in our land we have the novel and frightening sense that this continent may be the continent of yesterday; Africa and Asia are tomorrow's worlds. We look out of our windows and see only peaceful suburbia, but the view is dangerously deceptive. I have often sat, as I am sure you have, in a plane at 39,000 feet and watched the sun on the wing. It is warm and quiet and pleasant on our side of the triple plexiglass, and the tapering riveted expanse of aluminum wing looks so warm and quiet that we might picture ourselves sun-bathing on it. But of course it is 69.5 degrees below zero out there, and across that surface a subsonic blast is ripping at nearly six hundred miles an hour. The chill factor is such that death would be a matter of seconds to the most warmly dressed person. So is the turbulence of our times a killing thing. It is not alone on Coyote Dry Lake that such lethal whirling exists.

The dust devils of the dry lake were not only the products of aridity and turbulence, they were marked by impermanence. I do not know how long they lasted. They rose high into the pale sky above the salt lake when I stopped to look, but when I returned a few hours later their spectral march across the white flats had ceased. There are some phenomena of nature which are marked by the quality of duration—the everlasting hills, the cycle of day and night, and the ever returning tides—but the dust devils are creatures ephemeral and episodic. And again we have a similarity to the social conditions of our times, for there is little therein that is lasting and stable. Since I am leaning on poetry rather heavily this morning I continue by quoting that great poet of the desert, Omar Khayyam, who tells of the folly of ambition and the brevity of achievement in a familiar quatrain.

> The worldly hope men set their hearts upon,
> Turns ashes, or it prospers, and anon,
> Like snow upon the desert's dusty face,
> Lighting a little hour or two, is gone.

Not only do our material possessions have a quality of vanishment, but even when we keep the bare physical possession, the desire that made it meaningful departs. I have stashed by the head of my bed a violin case, and in it is a rather good fiddle which, some fifty years ago, I scrimped and sacrificed to buy. And for years it gave me a delight quite out of proportion to the skill with which it was played. But now arthritic fingers will not bend so much as to play "Happy Birthday to You" at family occasions, and the tail-piece has pulled out. And to get into the interiority of the matter, I really don't miss it. It had its day and ceased to be as an object of desire or joy, and I am sure that each one of you, out of personal experience can think of like instances—the object of desire is perhaps broken, is still had or lost or gone, or remains whole, but the desire itself has died. Darkly true are the somber words of Scripture: ". . . the world passeth away and the lust thereof."

And now having considered the short strange dance of the dust devils and used them for figures and parables, let us consider their relevance to the partaking of the Lord's Supper, for there is a very real and pertinent set of truths to be drawn from my basic metaphor. If the ghostly whirls of salt sand are symbols of aridity, turbulence, and impermanence, the reality of Christ's table is marked by the opposite qualities of life-giving water, peace, and permanence. The Old Testament Scriptures, being written by men whose God came to them in the desert of the Sinai Peninsula, abound in reference to the need for water. Their pilgrimage to liberty was marked by stages of journeying from well to meager well across that barren land. The old covenant tells of how their great leader, Moses, smote a stone and produced a gushing spring, and the New Testament records the act saying "He gave them water out of the rock." The returning exiles from Babylon, after traversing the wastes of the Arabian Desert, were invited to drink by the prophet Isaiah, "Ho, every one that thirsteth, come ye to the waters." How rich and splendid are the words of Christ to the life-battered woman by the well of Sychar: "Jesus answered and said unto her, whosoever drinketh of this water shall thirst again; but whosoever drinketh of the water that I shall give him shall never thirst, but the water that I shall give him shall be in him a well of water springing up into everlasting life." Water is an essential of life physical and spiritual, without water the land dies of thirst; without the water of the Spirit the soul of man dies. The analogies are many beyond our power to explicate now, but when you partake of the cup at the table, remember that it is not the sip of wine or grape juice that is the essence of our drinking, but the spiritual partaking of the water of life. If your life is marked by aridity, if you are walking a devil-haunted path through dry places, come to this table and drink, and your immortal thirst will be quenched.

And there is peace at this table. I speak now not of the great sociological storms that are raging across the earth in this century of change, but rather of those interior gales that howl within the single soul, unheard by others, but, nevertheless, a swirl and tumult of emotion that shakes the tempest-tossed heart. Rare is that one of us who does not know at times inner turbulence—desire, fear, uncertainity—all the familiar gusts of emotion that strew the interior landscape with wreckage, and are deadly foes of inner quiet. I do not say that the Lord's Table is the only place of peace; the garden of prayer is such a refuge; but they who sit at the Supper have great peace within. If there is one here (and I am sure that there is more than one, people being what they are and life being what it is) who has turbulence within, I say to you, "Partake in faith, and the tempest of the heart will subside as the midnight storm on Galilee quieted at the Master's word, and a great calm will come."

And here we leave the world of transient things and find permanence. The possessions of this world are lost or outgrown or stolen from us, but the spirit's havings are timeless and untakable. This is what Jesus meant when he told those gathered by him on the Mount: "Lay not up for yourselves treasures upon earth, where moth and rust doth corrupt and thieves break through and steal; But lay up for yourselves treasure in heaven, where neither moth nor rust doth corrupt and where thieves do not break through nor steal." The material possessions of this world are inherently transitory, and even the greatest of secular bards tells us:

> . . . like the baseless fabric of this vision,
> The cloud-capp'd towers, the gorgeous palaces,
> The solemn temples, the great globe itself,
> Yea, all which it inherit, shall dissolve
> And, like this insubstantial pageant faded,
> Leave not a track behind.

But these are things seen, and so temporal. Whoever comes to this table in trust, sees the unseen Host, and in communion with him touches the eternal. For Christ's great Supper deals with the realities that fade not nor pass away, because they are of God, The Eternal, who is from everlasting to everlasting.

—*Congregational Church of the Messiah, 1976.*

## 21

## A Fire, a Gun, and the High Stars

> The Lord is my light and my salvation; whom shall
> I fear? The Lord is the strength of my life, of whom
> shall I be afraid?
>
> *Psalm 27:1*

On a May midnight this spring, I sat by a small fire not far east of the ghost town of Ballarat in Panamint Valley. My son was asleep in my pickup truck, and, as is my custom, I was feeding on the silence, the night, the emptiness. The solitude was not quite as complete as I would have liked. Less than a mile away, on the dirt road that parallels the Trona-Grapevine Road, a brace of campers had pulled off to spend the night. But their lights were out now, and the Death Valley traffic had thinned out. Except for a couple of headlights crawling down Rt 190 toward Panamint Springs twenty miles away, I had the night pretty much to myself. I like Panamint Valley. It lacks the grandeur of its neighbor to the east, and it has no such visual glamour as Butte Valley has, nor is it as isolated as Eureka Valley with its tall, golden dunes and the great broad scar of white ledge in the last Chance Range behind them, but it has its own charm. As you move up the hill from Trona and come out onto the vista of Panamint Valley, its gray immensity, suddenly seen, has a powerful visual impact. Russ Leadabrand, whose back-country pieces in *Westways* first got me interested in the dirt roads of California, says that the valley is haunted: in no other place is there such a brooding sense of the continuing presence of "the Old Ones" as in this deserted valley that runs the length of the western side of the Panamint Mountains. I never had any psychic experiences in my nights in Panamint Valley, though I have often thought of that strange, tough little prospector, Shorty Harris, who was all that that flamboyant prevaricator, Death Valley Scotty, claimed to be in the way of gold hunter and wanderer of the wastelands.

So I sat there with the world to myself. There was no moon, the stars were big, and they came down to the jagged western horizon—the Argus Range and Wild Horse Mesa. The night was chilly, and though I was well wrapped up, the fire, an intense mass of glowing charcoal with but little flame, gave me pleasant warmth and a bit of light. My constant travel companion in journeying in places of loneliness, snakes, and possible bad men—a .22 magnum Deringer—lay on my table, near at hand. And suddenly, as not infrequently happens in such midnight musing, a sermon was born. The small hot fire, the potent little gun, and the glorious company of the high stars were instantly linked in a thought for preaching. Man is a weak creature; he needs protection. That is the simple theme of today's sermon. We dwell in the midst of hostile or lethally indifferent forces, and apart from protection our lives are vulnerable and short.

Consider first the fire. Fire is sunshine that shone a long yesterday ago. It was caught as wood, or coal, or gas, and makes a night of now into day, or at least chases the gloom far enough so that there is a magic circle of light in which we are safe from fear. Thomas Hobbes' familiar quotation dealing with the life of man in a state of nature is chiefly known for its harsh adjectives—"nasty, poor, brutish, and short." But it was also marked, as the philosopher noted, by "continual fear." Fire helped primitive man lessen that fear. When I was a youngster Kipling's jungle stories intrigued me, and one scene stays vividly in mind. The animals on Council Rock are terrified when Shere Khan, the great tiger, appears; even Bagheera, the black panther, and Alekah, chief of the wolves, are uneasy. But Mowgli, the man-cub, boldly lights a branch from the council fire and thrusts it into the face of the snarling but cowed lord of the jungle. The cave man went in fear of the great saber-toothed cat, but when some nameless benefactor of the race, in an infinite yesterday, put fire to use as a weapon, the great predators, still deadly, were no longer absolute monarchs of the night. Fire also protected man from the cold. As the great glaciers ground inexorably southward and the winters were longer and more cruel, the fire in the cave's front held killing frost at bay. But fire was more than heat; it was light, and the awesome darkness of the night, full of evil noises and lurking horrors, was made bearable by the ring of light which came from the friendly blaze. In a sense we are yet children of the cave man, for night and darkness still bring atavistic fears to make the heart pound and breath stop at the sound of a noise which would be unheeded by day. The light switch—a refinement of firelight—saves modern men and women from the terror that the old Scottish rhyme tells:

> From ghoulies and ghosties,
> Long leggity beasties,
> And things that go bump in the night,
> Good Lord, deliver us.

The Greeks, who truly do have a word and a tale for everything, tell us that when Prometheus, taking pity on man, stole fire, until then the sole property of the Olympians, and gave it to man, the gods were so furious with him for thus raising man nearer to them, that they chained him to a rock where vultures perpetually tear at his liver. Fire is a great protector; beasts, cold, and the terrible dark are lessened by it.

Fire, therefore, is a symbol of man's need for protection from the primal fears of beasts, cold, and dark. The gun is a bit more sophisticated sort of protection. It may be that you are either surprised or shocked by the thought that a minister of the Gospel should be carrying a lethal weapon. I once wrote a long, carefully documented thesis on the ethics of carrying weapons from the standpoint of the Judeo-Christian tradition; the study was based on the data in the Bible. Firearms are not mentioned in Scripture, of course. The only place a word suggesting the use of gunpowder in the Scriptures is to be found in I Samuel 20:40, "And Jonathan gave his artillery unto his lad," but this merely means his bow and arrows. The basis of my reasoning was that death can be inflicted by a stone or club or knife, just as well as by a rifle. So I studiously looked up every sort of lethal arm—sword, spear, arrow, dagger, sling, axe—all of which I considered to be the moral equivalents of a gun. After studying the data, I came to the conclusion that while both the Old and New Testaments are opposed to war and the promiscuous shedding of blood, the bearing of arms for personal defense is nowhere prohibited. Indeed, there is that perplexing passage in Luke (22:35-38) in which Jesus tells the disciples, "... He that hath no sword, let him sell his garment, and buy one." And an equally complex passage, upon which exegetes have labored, is the one in which Peter defends Christ in the Garden by cutting off the ear of the servant of the high priest. It's too long to analyze here, but the point is that Peter, apparently in obedience to Christ's earlier command, had bought a sword and was ready to wield it defensively. The whole business of the right of a citizen to bear arms, and the social evil of many murders by gunfire, is hotly debated in our time; one point of a single sermon is not room enough for a comprehensive treatment of an intricate issue. I happen to be in favor of the California law which permits the sale of registered hand guns to persons with no criminal record. And while the tale would be over-long and over-lurid for pulpit use, once, about a dozen years ago, on a lonely desert road, I was menaced by what I am forced to conclude was none other than Charlie Manson and three of his boys. And did I not have a pistol, the gift of my wife, it is entirely possible that I would have taken the place of the dead ravished girl who was found in that area a few days later.

But I must not overlook the main symbolism of the gun on the table by the campfire. As the fire was protection from inimical natural forces, the gun is a protection from hostile men. It is not a pleasant truth, but our safety (and it lessens night by night in these evil times) in many ways depends on the pistol on the policeman's hip. In an imperfect world, we must make an appeal to force. We cannot be pure above the world. This is why, despite the earnest and sincere efforts of pacifists, nations continue to arm themselves. It is a grim testimony to the depravity of man, that historically no nation has survived after it lost the will and the ability to defend itself. The Army, as costly, as wasteful, as it is, is society's gun. I wish and pray for a world in which men shall have beaten their swords into ploughshares and their spears into pruning hooks, but as I see it, that time is not now, and I am more realist than idealist. I recently heard Harry Jaffa, professor of history at Claremont, say a sad but accurate thing, "Many Americans do not realize that there are more people in the world who want us dead than who want us alive." Until the good day of universal brotherhood shall dawn, while ever striving to make this a free world, we must realize that for our protection we need a gun, be that weapon the lightest rifle or the dirtiest nuclear bomb.

The fire for protection from the dark forces of nature; the gun for protection from evil men. But let a man be warmly housed where beast cannot fang him; let the Maginot Line of his night table hold that which deals death to rapist or robber; still he is not wholly safe. He needs protection against sin and evil. By sin I mean that badness which comes by free choice out of man's wicked heart. By evil I mean that which comes on him from without—sickness, accident, all manner of external disaster. Against these ills he needs the protection of Almighty God. In our metaphor this morning God is symbolized by the high stars. As I sat there in the growing chill of the post-midnight air, my fire sinking to embers, I looked up at the incomparable pageantry of the stars—the blurred cluster of the Pleiades, warrior Orion with his belt and sword, the Big Dipper wheeling majestically around steadfast Polaris, and the westering whiteness of the Milky Way, inconceivably distant, inconceivably multitudinous—and to my lips there came the Psalmist's lyric cry:

> When I consider thy heavens, the work of thy fingers,
> the moon and the stars, which thou hast ordained:
> what is man that thou art mindful of him, and the son
> of man that thou visitest him?

And that God is mindful of us, and that he does visit us, is our true shield against all manner of evil, be it from within or from without; be it of meaning in this world or the next.

There is no security apart from God, and all the devices by which men and women seek safety are but toys. To be sure, it is well to take precautions where we can. Work hard and get a sure position in your firm; keep your social contacts in good order; watch your weight and pay attention to what the doctor tells you; have the good defense of a loving family. These are sound precepts and will doubtless make for a longer and a happier life. Such precautions are fences against prowling adversaries. But total protection? No thinking person ever assumes that. We are terribly vulnerable creatures and as we get older our vulnerability becomes ever more apparent and terrifying. A bubble of air in an artery, a slippery bathtub, a wild cell in brain or pancreas, and all our wise precautions are in vain. Nor does our state in life make much difference. Banker or beggar, preacher or gangster, socialite or back street nobody, famous or unknown, time and chance happeneth to us all. The low and humble, the high and mighty are alike defenseless. *King Richard the Second* isn't one of Shakespeare's best, but there is a poignant passage in that play which tells of the disposition and death of that monarch, mismatched against strong, savage barons and dukes. Now it must be kept in mind, if this passage is to be seen in its emotional perspective, that to the Elizabethan of Shakespeare's time a king was more than mortal; the divine right of kings was no empty phrase; the king was God's vice-regent on earth; he was not as other men. He was seemingly secure, hedged about by all manner of earthly guards. So there is horror, shock, in seeing a king brought to helplessness. In a lonely place on the coast of Wales, weak Richard learns that his arch-foe, cruel Bolingbroke, is victorious, and, sensing the nearness of disposition and death, Richard cries:

> For God's sake, let us sit upon the ground
> And tell sad stories of the death of kings:
> How some have been depos'd; some slain in war,
> Some haunted by the ghosts they have depos'd;
> Some poison'd by their wives; some sleeping kill'd;
> All murder'd; for within the hollow crown

> That rounds the mortal temples of a king
> Keeps Death his court, and there the antic sits,
> Scoffing his state and grinning at his pomp,
> Allowing him a breath, a little scene,
> To monarchize, be fear'd and kill with looks,
> Infusing him with self and vain conceit,
> As if this flesh which walls about our life
> Were brass impregnable, and humour'd thus
> Comes at the last and with a little pin
> Bores through his castle wall, and farewell king!

Consider, if you will, the burning brilliance of Shakespeare's genius in his choice of the tool that penetrates the royal protection. It isn't a great sword, or a heavy axe, or a long spear, or a ponderous mace; it's a little pin—a two-inch sliver of steel. And it tells with fearful clarity the fragility of us all. Each of us, like the wretched king, can be slain by some little pin of disease or accident.

But while we stand in need of protection from the evils from without, there is another foe of man, less dramatic but no less—nay, even more—deadly. That is *sin*, the evil from within. It is the wrong which we willingly do, not that crash of brute event that comes without our volition, that is the more perilous. We have souls as well as bodies, and our awesome power of free choice, wrongly exercised, can damage our souls as devastatingly as accident or cancer can harm our flesh. The hot rush of passion, the icy prison of malice, the powerful tide of greed, are evils from inside, and there are times when our discipline, or our desire to do what we should do, is overmatched by them. It is then that we need God's help, and it is then that his will and purpose for each of us, as high and holy as the stars that burn above dark mountains and broad sea, is our true protection. By saying this I do not mean that the faithful believer will be spared all blows of fate or strokes of disease, or even wanderings from the path of righteousness. What I do mean is the truth that the noble pagan Socrates said to the judges who had sentenced him to death by drinking poison. "Know, O my judges, that there is nothing in heaven or earth can harm a good man"; it is the very truth that our text sings:

> The Lord is my light and my salvation; whom shall I
> fear? The Lord is the light of my life, of whom shall
> I be afraid?

It is the sweet truth that pervades the magnificent 91st Psalm.

> He that dwelleth in the secret place of the most high
> shall abide under the shadow of the Almighty. I will
> say of the Lord, he is my refuge and my fortress: my
> God, in him will I trust. Surely he shall deliver you . . .

It is the truth by which Christ lived and died and lived again, for when the twelve legions of angels his Father had the power to give him for his protection against his foes and the cross did not come, he nevertheless found in God's high and shining will for him the strength that enabled him to commit his spirit into his Father's hands and to experience the ultimate protection that prevailed over evil and death. And there are those who sit here this morning who share with Christ and his saints of the past and present the conviction that whosoever trusts in God's abiding love is safe from all dangers which can hurt the body and harm the soul.

These are some of the thoughts that came to me as I sat solitary in the darkness of a great ghostly valley, my puny helps of fire and gun at hand, and overhead the great high stars that spoke without words of God.
—*First Congregational Church of Los Angeles, 1980.*

## 22

## Short View from Skiddoo

When there is no vision, the people perish.
*Proverbs 29:18*

On a bright, warm March morning last year, I turned off the pavement of the Emigrant Canyon Road into Death Valley onto the dirt road that leads to the long-vanished ghost town of Skiddoo. It was a pleasant ride on a twisting trail that led up easy grades and through shallow canyons to the bowl in the hills, pock-marked by the openings and tailings of abandoned mine shafts, which was the site of that raucous town. Skiddoo was started in 1906 by two prospectors who were lost in the fog (there are desert fogs), and the ledge they found next morning soon brought a gold rush in the place. It was an enterprising group of miners, for when water proved in short supply, they ran a flume from the snowy top of Telescope Peak, 23 miles away, from which distance the town got its name. And there may be those listening who remember the cryptic slang expression, "Twenty-Three Skiddoo."

The scene was superb. Not a stick remained standing of the buildings, but one could look westward and northwestward across the intervening summits of the Panamint Range and the Inyo Mountains, and see, over the golden hills in the foreground, silver in the sun, the needle teeth of Mt. Whitney sharp against the clean blue sky of morning.

We read the information on the sign erected by the Forestry Service, and we read also the grimy saga of Joe "Hooch" Simpson, a dim-witted drunkard who killed kindly Jim Arnold, the local bank manager, and of the revenge Jim's friends took. The whole tale is complicated and bizarre, and in addition to being grisly is very likely somewhat contrived, and, therefore, not profitable for pulpit telling. But both my son and I were interested in the more prosaic matters of the life of Skiddoo—it lasted only eleven years. In its glory days, the board read, Skiddoo had a population of 700, and not one, but two newspapers, three restaurants, two roominghouses, three saloons, a telephone line to Rhyolite, a hardware store, and a bank. I said to my son, "What's missing?" and answered my own question, "No churches, and no schools." His response capped the observation perfectly. "And no future," he said.

And that's where the theme of this sermon is to be found. The physical view from that vanished town was long and lovely, but the social and spiritual view was short and drab. The men who came to Skiddoo came for a quick run at gold and silver; they did not come to make a place of dwellings. They did not erect a school; they did not build a church. Their views, both of this world and the next, and of the town which became a ghost in 1917, were short. So we go to the serious theme of this sermon. America's greatness and survival has been based in long measure on the fact that its early settlers found places for education and religion. Theirs was the long view that includes the school house and the place of worship. And as a second fugal statement in this sermonic two-part invention, let it be said that the individual who has a long view of life will constantly go on reading and praying.

Education and religion are closely linked in their origins. The word "hieroglyphics," that is, the characters by which ancient Egyptians expressed themselves, comes from two Greek roots, "hieros"—sacred or priestly—and "glyphe"—a carving—a clear indication that literacy and religion are related. It is a little known but highly significant fact that our whole American ideal of universal literacy, indeed, that of our whole western culture, has a religious origin. Up until the year 1500, salvation depended simply upon accepting what Mother Church taught. From the priest's sermon or from the stories of the Bible as they were seen in stained glass windows, or from the teaching of Holy Church, unquestioningly accepted, came salvation. But Martin Luther, that giant figure, changed all that. He taught the right of private judgment, which, said technically, meant that the Holy Spirit would instruct the seeker how to read the Bible aright in all the things necessary for salvation. Well, in order to read the Bible you must, of course, be able to read, and in that age of beautiful rare hand-written Bibles, there was little chance of common folk ever seeing a Bible, let alone having the skill to read one. But by a remarkable coincidence, just when there was an enormous social imperative for literacy, Johann Gutenberg (his real name was Gensfleisch) invented movable type, and the first printed book, the superlative Gutenberg Bible, appeared, soon to be followed by many less beautiful but more available versions. One would never guess it to survey the Los Angeles school system today, but education sprang from the soil of faith in God, and the need for salvation. Our own branch of Protestantism carried this joint zeal for learning and religion to the New World. Familiar is the fact that John Harvard, a Congregational minister, left fifty pounds and a number of books to found Harvard's present enormous endowment, and the college itself bore witness to our concern for a learned ministry—"Dreading to leave an illiterate ministry to posterity when our present godly ministers are dust." Less known is the fact that on the common in Dedham, Massachusetts, there is a small bronze marker saying that on this spot in 1644 stood the first tax-supported common school in America. I have often looked on it with pride and appreciation as one of the unheralded but significant contributions of our way of church life to our way of national life.

But in the last forty years there has been a change, and a change by no means for the better. I cannot state the exact causes of this deleterious alteration. I once attributed it to the influence of John Dewey, but two teachers screamed so wildly that I have eased off that theory. Whatever the underlying causes may be, certainly education in the classical sense has suffered severe damage, damage sufficient to make even the contributors to *Saturday Review* note the disintegration with alarm. To take but one discipline—language. Slovenly style is rampant. The new doctrine that usage by the many, unbalanced by the usage by the masters, is the sole criteria of acceptance, has appalling results. The much-asked question, "Why can't Johnny read?" has been drowned by a chorus showing that it really isn't necessary for him to read. As a result, we have a terrifying amount of actual illiteracy in our school systems. The child who doesn't learn to read in the early grades is given what I believe is called "social promotion," and he goes right on up the grade ladder. I do not have the figures at hand, but I am sure that many of you read the recent account in the *Los Angeles Times* describing the educational shambles at Jefferson High School. On any given day half the pupils are absent, but the process of promotion goes on, in part, I suppose, because authorities don't know what else to do.

But we have the sad result that there are students in local junior colleges who literally can't read. I know of a professor in a Los Angeles city college who said that even when he had cut down the home work of his class in English literature to one short story a week, a committee from the class approached him and asked him if he would not read the story aloud to them in class time. But I would not have you think that I am lamenting the process of non-education only as it obtains in the inner city.

Not long ago, a friend of mine, a teacher himself, a high school principal in a New England town, told me that I was behind the times in my insistence that the ability to read was necessary. His wife triumphantly cited what she had done in educating her third (or maybe it was her second grade) class. They had put on a cookie sale in front of the Town Hall. I looked puzzled. "Don't you see the educational values?" she asked. "Look, it taught family relationships: the kids had to ask their mothers to bake the cookies. It taught civics: they had to get a permit at Town Hall to hold a sidewalk sale. It taught public relations: they had to be pleasant to people so that they would buy. It taught arithmetic: they had to count the number of cookies and make change. So you see how important it all was."

Faced by this fluent rationale I could only mumble. I didn't say what I really thought! "Ruth, it still seems like a cookie sale to me." Well, there's much more that could be said. I could speak of the rise and the apparent fall of the new math, of how the tube has taken away the joy of reading, of how the words in the comic strip are about all that gets read. The old hard disciplines of the three R's—"readin', 'ritin', and 'rithmetic" —are not much in fashion these days. Of course, if the prophecy of Arthur C. Clark, that giant of scientific fiction writers, who as long ago as 1945 described satellite communication and said that global pictures would soon supersede the printed word for much of mankind, is a true prophecy, reading will once again be a skill solely for the specialist. I hope he is a bad prophet. (*Harpers*, January 1962)

Not only has formal education fallen on hard times in these days, but so has formal religion. On the Friday morning that I was writing this sermon, the Los Angeles *Herald Examiner* offered a special section called Week End Style; its forty-four pages were devoted to news of the entertainment world—rock and country western music, the movies, the dance, theatre, sound, TV, and radio. I then went back to look at the rest of the paper; there was not a single line or a word that could be construed as coverage of religion, not even a terse item saying that the Pope had appointed a new bishop *in partibus infidelum* for Outer Mongolia. This is too narrowly based to be a wholly fair comment; on Saturday there would doubtless have been a bit more religious news, but the disproportion is significant.

It isn't the whole truth, but it is truth; it's admittedly a caricature, but caricature always has a point. Beyond the shadow of a doubt, American society in our day has been thoroughly secularized. Possibly Rome at the height of her decadence, and Byzantium before the hordes of Islam took her, may have been more engrossed in games and chariot races than we are in entertainment and Monday night football, the point could be sharply debated. But a new de Tocqueville, looking at us now would not find, as Count Alexis did a century and a half ago, that the secret of America's strength was her Churches. I do not mean to say that America is now godless; that would be a slander against the millions of earnest and simple believers who daily lift hands of prayer and try to follow Christ. It would fail to recognize the thousands of small Churches where the Word is preached and the sacraments observed week after week. But I do say that what catches public attention today are such figures as Jerry Falwell with his politically potent electronic Church, or Bob Schuller with his magnificent Crystal Cathedral. Indubitably the attention of most Americans is more directed to things of earth and fame than to the things of God as the Church of Christ proclaims them. It is something that Americans who are concerned about our survival as a major power need to think about and pray about. It is still terrifyingly true that where there is no vision the people perish; we are no more exempt from that law than were Rome and Byzantium. In our origin and in our growth we were a nation who at least said that we wanted to be a God-fearing people, whether we made it or not. We then had the long view that God had a plan for America, and that we were a people with a high destiny.

Let me now move abruptly from things of wide social and political nature to a bit of parochial fact in which we can take pride. First Congregation Church and Pilgrim School together exemplify the forces of institutions which gave America a long view and ensured her future. Education and religion have embraced each other in our parish as in few other places. The far sightedness of Dr. James Fifield and the generosity of Mr. and Mrs. Frank Seaver joined hands to bless us with this rare linkage of chuch and school. Both bodies have strands of patriotism and fibers of learning and worship which make for strength and continuance. Pilgrim School is a no-nonsense institution. It stands for the fundamentals—the simple things that are the foundations of literacy, not the fads and trends which have enervated many schools, but the strong disciplines of the classical curriculum—reading, writing, and arithmetic—and the solid studies—geography, physics, history. For this reason many parents who covet for their children a sound and useful education are making financial sacrifices to send their children to Pilgrim School for the basics of education. I have heard Mr. Philip Nordeck speak twice; each time I have been impressed, not only with the educational stresses the school is making under his leadership, but his advocacy of those other values which ought to be cherished—the Puritan ethic and a love of the American way of life. First Church has sometimes been criticized for being jingoistic, chauvinistic, in its approach to social goals. But I confess to you, although it seemed strange to me at first, that there is something meaningful in the singing of the last verse of "America" at the end of every service. We are still a great nation, and for all our faults we are still the country that refugees from other lands seek to reach. Russia is hailed by many as the promised land of tomorrow, but while American democracy has its deep flaws, and while our freedom is less than perfect, we never had to build a wall around our nation to keep people in. But I walk too wide afield, it is enough to say at First Church we are not like unschooled and churchless Skiddoo of the short view; and if we are true to our vision, we will not perish.

I have spent over-long with the corporate aspects of our theme to avoid an asymetrical discourse, for there is a personal theme in this morning's fugue: education and religion will give each of us a long view of life. Concludingly I'm going to be shamelessly personal in my treatment, and deliberately narrow our terms. I'm going to tell you of what reading and prayer have meant in my life. I literally cannot remember when I learned to read, or when I first went to Sunday School. I can remember surprising my teacher in the second grade by my facility in reading. It was about that age I used to go into the Beverly Public Library and read *St. Nicholas*, and systematically plough through the juvenile shelves until I almost ruined my eyes. I early learned the meaning of Emily Dickinson's couplet:

> There is no frigate like a book
> To take us lands away.

Reading is a form of education we can carry on for ourselves when we are no longer within college walls, reading is an anodyne for pain, reading is an excited treading of the paths of the mind where good guides have gone before us. I find that one of the deep satisfactions of my present life is the time I have to read. When I was a hard-working parish minister, I used to read, and read much, but I often had to steal the time, and I was not without guilt in my indulgence. Now I have long hours to turn pages, some frivolous, some profound, some pleasurably carnal, some demanding, but all helping to give me a longer and wider look at life. I say to you of all ages, young and old, reading is a form of education that is a source of unending delight. Read and your mind will not perish. I cannot help but think, although the Bible gives me no specific testimony, that the reason why Jesus at twelve answered the learned doctors so well was that he had spent long hours in reading, learning, and inwardly digesting Torah.

And as reading makes for a long look of the mind, so prayer lengthens the soul's vision. We have three sorts of seeing, for we are complex creatures of flesh, mind, and soul. I have touched upon the mind's seeing, I now speak of the other two sorts. In the brilliant spring sunshine I stood on the site of Skiddoo and saw the ranges receding into the west, Panamint, Inyo, and Sierra. Should I stand there at night the low steady planets would shine and the high stars twinkle, and with a good pair of binoculars I could study interesting things—the mountains and craters of the moon, the rings around Saturn, the Pleiades changing from blur to seven-fold clarity. But an astronomer with great optical and radio telescopes at his command could peer yet more deeply into the abysses of outer space. Or, to change directions, the viewer with magnifying glass or microscope could bring very small things up to visibility. For his skilled use are available instruments of magnification so potent that infinitesimal viruses become swimming monsters. But these intricate machines of viewing are only extensions of the physical power; they bring the world of matter into clarity of view. But there is another world—the spiritual—and in that world polished lenses and vast concave mirrors are useless.

> Let the bacteriologist look inward with the best of tools, there are things he cannot see.
> Let the astronomer point Palomar's giant scope toward the far frontiers of space, and stare till his mind wearies,
> There is Someone he will not see.
> There are realities and beings visible only to the soul, and the soul has an indispensable aid to seeing.
> It is called prayer.
> Without that aid man gropes blindly toward death:
> His vision of ultimate reality is short and dim; he will perish.
> Happy are those who look with the eyes of prayer.
> Blessed are those who pray, for they shall see God, and live.
> —*First Congregational Church of Los Angeles, 1980.*

# 23

# Campfire at Greenwater: The Vanity of Human Hopes

Vanity of vanities, saith the preacher... all is vanity.
*Ecclesiastes 1:2*

And I, John, saw the holy city, new Jerusalem, coming down from God out of heaven, prepared as a bride adorned for her husband.
*Revelation 21:2*

The thesis for our thinking this morning is that all human dreams, even the best, have a transient quality: only the hopes that are grounded in God are permanent.

On a bright winter's morning when the chill was going out of the desert air, I was driving along a seldom-travelled road that runs from Shoshone to Death Valley, my son Jack at my side. It is a thirty-mile stretch up the Greenwater Valley and the first eleven miles are miserable by reason of the number of washes that must be crept across, and the rocks that bestrew the unmaintained road. It isn't dangerous; it's just slow, jolty going. Late last November we had lurched up that trail with dark coming down and had not realized that off to our left was the ghost town of Greenwater. Returning home, I had read of the town in an account which said, "There miners rushed to what promoters advertised as the greatest copper camp on earth, but the hopeful, the gullible, and the drifters were left with little to do but nurse their futile dreams... not a single one of the 2,500 recorded claims brought in anything worthwhile. But the town, whose population grew to about a thousand, had several saloons, stores, a bank, a post office, two newspapers, and even telephone service. It also had its share of shenanigans and shootouts." Historian Harold Weight notes that "after the death of Billy Robinson following a prolonged binge . . . the saints, the sinners, and the inbetweens all attended Billy's rites, and Tiger Lil placed five aces in his hand, pressed close to his breast, 'so he'll look natural.' "

Obviously, this was a town worth visiting, and after carefully reading the tenths of miles between trails indicated by the Auto Club map, we drove along a smooth road through the chaparral on the easy slopes of the Black Mountains. But there was nothing but sage in sight.

"Where's the town?" asked my son.

And I said, "We are in it."

At the crossroads was a post, and on it a recent sign saying "Greenwater, 4380," and a number of refreshingly nonobscene graffiti—"Tom and Bill and Ed wasted their time and gas coming to this place," "The night life here is not riotous," and my son added the words, "Greenwater, room for 250,000. Bring your own water." We went up the road to Greenwater Spring, a drop-by-drop trickle from a rusty pipe, and came back to town to make camp for the night. I say town, but there was absolutely nothing standing. All through the brush were strewn the boards, and beams, and clapboards of old houses demolished by the rains and winds. There were rusty kerosene cans, and, interestingly, many vestiges of old hand-cranked telephone batteries—carbon rods with a little zinc paste left on them. So after clearing the truck and gathering wood against the coming night, I went for a walk. I climbed a knoll and looked out on the empty and beautiful valley. To the east lay the Greenwater Mountains, to the west the Black Mountains that stand over southern Death Valley. Far, far to the north and blued by distance, stood the Last Chance Range, and to the southeast were the snow-crowned summits of the Spring Range in Nevada. Save for a faint yellow tracery of sand roads through the green chaparral, there was no sign of man's handiwork. The valley was clean, empty, as serene as it was ten thousand years ago. I thought of the vanished town, and the familiar lines of Shelley came to my lips:

> I met a traveler from an antique land
> Who said: "Two vast and trunkless legs of stone
> Stand in the desert. Near them, on the sand

(continues the poet, by an empty pedestal, lay the battered visage of an ancient and cruel king.)

> And on the pedestal these words appear:
> 'My name is Ozymandias, king of kings:

> Look upon my works, ye Mighty, and despair:'
> Nothing beside remains. Round the decay
> Of that colossal wreck, boundless and bare
> The lone and level sands stretch far away.

But even as I spoke these stately words over the place where once Greenwater had been, I realized that they didn't precisely say what I was groping for. Shelley was writing about the ends of empires and the destruction of dynasties, which was a little florid for a threnody over a town that only lasted from 1903 to 1906. I eased my way down the slopes and trudged back to camp, flushing two big jack rabbits who were abroad as the sun sank.

The homiletic problem still haunted me as the great desert stars blossomed in the cloud-clear sky and to the southeast the loom of Las Vegas, a hundred miles away, was like the light that goes before the rising moon. I don't go to the desert deliberately seeking sermon ideas, but I count that trip less than perfect when I don't stumble on one. I fed the campfire with more pieces of house wreckage and went for a walk to see if any ghosts were still alive in the town—I'm a true believer in psychic phenomena. But nothing was alive except the faint breeze that stirred the sage. Suddenly, as I put a piece of dark dessicated wood on the flames, I realized why "Ozymandias" didn't fit the emptiness of Greenwater Valley. The death of Greenwater wasn't a matter of "The Decline and Fall of the Roman Empire," or a Toynbeean crumbling of cultures. It was the short-lived and little-noted death of an insignificant boom town like hundreds of others in the American West. What was sermonically significant and different was that the tragedy wasn't the impermanence of a Pharaoh or a Caesar or a Napoleon; it was the breaking of the dreams of a few little, unremembered people who had pinned their hopes on striking it rich in this lonely and sterile valley. The piece of studding I had just put on the flame had been erected with who knows what confidence by some young business man. Who knows with what pride some enterprising editor cranked the phone powered by one of those batteries that now lay crumbled by the fireside? This piece of window sash might have held glass that was proudly curtained by some young wife who hoped to see Greenwater become a place of schools and churches where her children could be taught to read and worship. But their hopes and dreams were brief and broken, and their homes and offices were now fuel for a chance fire. As I visioned that vanished yesteryear, the campfire itself seemed to change; it was no longer a friendly thing—light in the darkness, warmth in the wind. It was a monster with yellow teeth and red gullet, dream-devourer, hope-eater. The rising wind whimpered through the brush, the uncaring mountains looked down on the emptiness, and in the mind of the preacher who sat pondering by the fire went the words of a greater preacher of long ago who told of the brevity and pointlessness of human aspiration, "Vanity of vanity, saith the preacher"—emptiness of emptiness, all is emptiness.

And it seemed to me as I sat there in icy breeze by the dying fire that the ghost town of Greenwater was a profound and subtle parable of the human condition apart from God. Who of us has not known the vanished dream, nor laid down at night with "the half of a broken hope for a pillow"? When we are young our dreams have vividness, color, certainty. Of course we are going to be elected queen of the prom, or man most likely to succeed. We are going to write stuff that sells; we will certainly have one of the finest homes in town; being president of the company is simply a matter of time. But the abrasive realities of life grind us down; the hostilities, the frustrations, the perversities of brute event destroy the dreams and make hopes dwindle, and the time all too soon comes when we are drab creatures, hoping only to survive, to get by, to be able to cope. "The destruction that wasteth at noonday"—middle age—has a way of diminishing hope to mere wishfulness. And it is a sad and true thing that sometimes, when we do get the hoped-for thing, or reach the place we dreamed of reaching, we discover that it wasn't worth it. Sometimes the realized human hope is even more tragic than the lost hope. With subtlety and insight does that great poet of futility, Omar Khayyam, say the acid truth:

> The worldly hope men set their hearts upon
> Turns ashes, or, it prospers, and anon,
> Like snow upon the desert's dusty face,
> Lighting a little hour or two, is gone.

And we must not suppose that the ephemeral dreams of those who tried vainly to make a place of habitation in Greenwater Valley, those unlucky dreamers who were there for short months, are the only men and women who have been victims of the passing nature of human hopes. The bravest and wisest and the best have had a like disenchantment. Columbus, dying in disgrace after seeking for the Indies and knowing the glory of being Admiral of the Ocean Sea; Socrates, after a lifetime of teaching and high example, drinking the poison prescribed by fellow Athenians who did not understand him; Joan of Arc, girl of faith and conqueror of the English invader, dying in the smoke and agony of a heretic's stake —all these are examples of the vanity of human yearnings. Nor may we strike Christ himself and his disciples from this roll. In the Church Calendar, next Sunday is Passion Sunday, and the following week is Passion

Week. These commemorate the days when Christ's hopes and those of his followers flamed highest. He was going up to Jerusalem, and while he had dark and bitter forebodings of what would happen to him at the hands of the rulers, irrational hope—the trust in his dream of Messiahship—still burned within him. Happy expectations were brightened by Palm Sunday, the day of the triumphal entry.

And yet it is clear to the careful reader of the Gospels that in the days immediately following Palm Sunday, Christ came to see that what he dreamed of—the earthly Messiahship—was not to be. For in the events and parables of the first three days of Holy Week, Christ's bitter disappointment rose up like a hot flood of anger. Gone were the sweet parables of love, and in their place grim tales of death and vengeance were spoken—one being about the treacherous farmers who killed even the son whom the lord sent to collect the rightful rent. The harsh "little apocalypse" poured from his lips. He called his foes vipers and wondered how they could escape the damnation of hell. He went into the temple and overthrew the tables of the money changers and scourged them with a whip of small cords. Most inexplicable of all, he even cursed a poor fig tree that lacked fruit when no fruit could be expected, so that it withered away. There is now no time to examine in detail the black rage that surged in Christ during those few days when the realization that his earthly hopes were in vain, his human dream vanished beyond recall, drowned his spirit in understandable resentment and bitterness. We note only that in contrast to it, the ultimate affirmation of trust—"not my will, but thine be done" made under the olives at midnight on Thursday—shines with a more-than-earthly glory. And the events of the big week, from Palm Sunday to Golgotha, stand as witness to the somber truth of the first half of our thesis—"all human dreams, even the best, have a transient quality."

But that's only the first half. For if you listened closely and remember well, you recall that I wrote in an escape clause, a way out of the pessimism and fatalism which such an arid and meager view of life would make inevitable. I added, "only the hopes that are grounded in God are permanent." Our second text is one of the Bible's many warrants for a hope that is more than human in its origin and force. The book of Revelation is a strange one, and there's a strain of wildness that runs through it, but there is also a crystal beauty in some of the visions of that volume. "And I, John, saw the holy city, new Jerusalem, coming down from God out of heaven, prepared as a bride adorned for her husband." Now there is in the book of Revelation a harsh angular counter melody which tells not of the birth of a city, but of a death. There is a savage beauty in the eighteenth chapter which opens with an angel of great power and glory, crying mightily with a strong voice and saying, "Babylon the great is fallen, is fallen." In that exalted taunt song the merchants who were enriched by the traffic of the wicked city weep and wail, saying, "Alas, that great city, that was clothed in fine linen and purple and scarlet and decked with gold and precious stones and pearls: for in one hour so great riches is come to naught... the voices of harpers and musicians... shall be heard no more at all in thee... the light of the candle shall be seen no more at all in thee: and the voice of the bridegroom and the bride shall be heard no more at all in thee." Now this Babylon over whose destruction John exults, is, of course, the city of Rome, queen of the seven hills, the throne of Nero, who drank the blood of the saints and burned them with fire, and it is a symbol of the destruction of all earthly metropoli. All shall perish, from Nineveh and Tyre and Xanadu, to Greenwater, and, in time, Los Angeles. All are built on human hopes and all at last shall vanish.

But the writers of the Bible are haunted by a dream of "A city that hath foundation whose builder and maker is God." "We have here no abiding city," says the writers of Hebrews, "we are pilgrims moving on to a better country." Even the holy city itself, earthly Jerusalem is not exempt from the common lot: "Jerusalem which now is," declares Paul, "is in bondage, but Jerusalem which is above, the mother of us all, is free." It is not the Jerusalem built by David that John sings, but the new Jerusalem which comes down out of heaven fresh from the hand of God. St. Augustine, brooding on the imminent fall of the Roman Empire, looks to *De Civitas Dei*—the City of God as the fulfillment of man's best hopes. And we still sing Bernard of Cluny's yearning and joyous hymn:

> Jerusalem the golden, with milk and honey blest,
> Beneath thy contemplation sink heart and voice oppressed.
> I know not, O I know not, what joys await us there;
> What radiancy of glory, what bliss beyond compare.
>
> They stand, those halls of Zion, all jubilant with song,
> And bright with many an angel, and all the martyr throng.
> The Prince is ever in them, the daylight is serene;
> The pastures of the Blessed are decked in glorious sheen.

The cities of this earth, be their spans measured in thousands of years, or less than ten—the Babylons and the Greenwaters—have "their little day and cease to be," but the city of God, the city of heavenly hope, the city of man's best dream, is eternal.

Now let me, too abruptly, perhaps, turn from the corporate to the personal, and speak not of cities, but of us, we who are dwellers in cities. Each of us here has hopes and dreams, and every one of us has seen some of these dreams die and hopes twitch and vanish like bursting bubbles. But this is, in part at least, because we are children of a secular age, and our dreams and hopes are of the earth, earthy. We are thing-minded and carnal, and our aspirations are of affluence and status. We do not heed Christ's warning, "Lay not up for yourselves treasures upon earth, where moth and rust doth corrupt and where thieves break through and steal. But lay up for yourselves treasures in heaven, where moth and rust do not corrupt, and where thieves do not break through and steal." Like the rich fool, we lay up treasure for ourselves, and "are not rich toward God." We play for mortal stakes, and

> At our backs we seem to hear
> Time's winged chariot hurrying near.

We are obsessed with earth and time, and we neglect heaven and eternity. I tell you that until you see yourself *sub specie aeternitatis*—under the aspect of eternity—you do not see yourself whole.

We are now but twenty-one days from Easter, the day in which we celebrate the demonstrated hope of life everlasting. Too much, I think, does the pulpit of our time deal with mortal problems and earthly achievement. We are bodies, to be sure, and we live in this real and often brutal earth. But we are also souls, and our true citizenship is in heaven. I am a man of some years. I have lived those years realistically, and the goals and ambitions and joys of this world have been a meaningful part of my living. But by God's grace I have never forgotten that while I have a body (once strong and quick, now far less so), I have also a soul. Like all men and women I have my disappointments, my vanished visions. I have lived in Greenwater. Yet I bear witness, and to it many of you who are faithful will say "Amen," that my hopes which were rooted in God have never failed: that the plans I essayed at the promptings of His will always somehow succeeded even in this earth of incompletions and broken arcs. And I have the firm faith that in heaven I will see the complete and perfect circle. Live then as though earth was much, but not all: live in the hope of heaven, which is of God. And if you so live, you will go from the Greenwaters of time to the new Jerusalem, which is eternal.

—*Penge Congregational Church, London, 1981.*

## 24

## Pete Aguereberry, Patron of the Arts

*He hath made every thing beautiful in his time.*
*Ecclesiastes 3:11*

Today I am going to indulge myself by giving you one of the homiletic delicacies which I have learned to prepare during the latter years of my ministry, that is, take some seemingly small episode which I have witnessed (commonly in the desert) and relate it to some significant religious or moral reality, although admittedly not a major theological theme. This invariably entails considerable narrative before the serious work of exposition begins.

I like to visit Death Valley, not the part that tourists travel (Stove Pipe Wells, Furnace Creek, and Scotty's Castle—though these are in truth worth seeing), but the remote areas behind the mountains, reachable only by four-wheel-drive or high clearance trucks. So one day a while ago I loaded up my pick-up camper, Excelsior (my wife so named it because, she says, the truck and I are always moving upward and onward), and took off for The Racetrack, a remote attraction I had never seen. The tourist slogan, "getting there is half the fun," is never more true than it is on excursions into the California back country. When I turn off Route 14 at what once was Wagon Wheel onto the scenic road to Death Valley, I slow to a forty-mile rate and drive with a ranging eye. After a dawdling day through Trona, past Ballarat, and into the valley by way of Wildrose Canyon, I reached Mesquite Spring, and settled in for the night. I went as far north as possible, pumped my camper to full height, made supper, and settled to watch the flaming west subside to embers. In the deep dusk before moonrise a little brown shadow scuttled by my feet—a kangaroo rat hunting crumbs, swift as thought (well, actually 17 feet a second). He was joined by another in a leaping, ballet-type battle. Replete with food and potables, I dozed in my chair and was awakened by the flood of brilliance of the almost full moon rising over the Grapevine Range, banishing the little crepuscular creatures and making a delicate nocturnal chiaroscuro of the great salt flats and grim mountains. Then to bed.

Next morning as the east was reddening, the moon was dramatically setting behind Tin Mountain. In minutes the sunrise exploded into a chromatic skyscape I cannot catch in words. There were odd little wings of clouds over the Grapevine Mountains, and with kaleidoscope speed they went from deep red to silver and pink, with applegreens, and pale but electric blues sweeping over to the orangy-gold that crowned the tall tops of the Cottonwood Mountains. To the north, over Nevada, round-topped gray clouds with incongruous, ragged bottoms trailed rain veils—an air-absorbed water that never reached the needy earth. I fancy myself as a wordman, with some facility in snaring natural beauty in a net of sentences. This time, I could only look at that gorgeous phantasmagoria and mutter helplessly—"O my, O my." Then a slow breakfast of the basics —coffee, bacon, eggs—quaffed and eaten while packing gear and getting ready to go along the back road to The Racetrack. Up at five, at seven I started off, and was told by the rangers that the snow was four feet deep on the Hunter Mountain Road beyond Harris Hill, and not to try it. So began a halcyon day, and if that word sounds a bit precious, let me tell you that it is very precise. It comes from the Greek word for kingfisher, and Greek folklore says that kingfishers only mate on the waves when sky and sea are at their peak of beauty. I won't attempt to describe at length

*Teakettle Junction*

the twenty-six mile stretch of dirt road that runs behind the Cottonwood Mountains, from Ubehebe to Teakettle Junction (once marked by two ancient teakettles and five battered, shot-perforated coffee pots, and now, alas, a naked post raped by vandals). Then down the long slow slope, so smooth and straight that it could be travelled in fifth gear, with the flat brown oval of The Racetrack at the end. The Racetrack is a strange dry lake, for on its surface are huge stones up to six hundred pounds in weight, and these boulders, when the rain has wet the clay and the strong drying winds blow, slide over the slippery surface leaving their trails as a proof of their peregrinations. Of great and splendidly lonesome Racetrack Valley, walled by brown and black mountains, snow-summitted; of the sculptured clouds in the cerulean sky; of the incomparable luxury of spacious solitude; and of the intriguing trail that led out of the basin and down into Saline Valley—eighty-seven miles of emptiness—I cannot now tell in detail, for I must hasten on to the esthetic climax of the day—the pièce de résistance that filled my hungry eyes—the view from Aguereberry Point.

The road that leads to it is forbiddingly marked "Four Wheel Drive Advisable," but it isn't really all that bad, simply narrow, and in a few points, seemingly straight up. I walked the last steep quarter mile to get the ache out of my legs and stepped out on the natural stone tower that juts out of the Panamint Range. There from an elevation of 6,400 feet I looked out on the whole magnificent 130-mile sweep of the deepest and dryest valley in America, from Confidence Hills far to the south, and the salt flats, bordered by Badwater and Shorty Harris' grave, over to Tucki Mountain and the gray sprawl of Emigrant Wash and the Dunes, to distant Ubehebe Crater. To the east lay the stark and treeless mountains —Greenwater Range, the Black Mountains, the Funeral Range, and the Grapevine Mountains. Against this awesome backdrop, the works of man—Stovepipe Wells and Furnace Creek villages—were dwarfed to near invisibility. But it was not only the vastness of the valley that stunned the senses, but the indescribable welter of color. Behind me were the gray-green undulations of the Emigrant Canyon graben, before me the iron-gray-and-black of the mountains, with the blending browns and reds of their gully-gashed foothills, and the white salt flats, all touched and intensified by the pink and gold light of the westering sun that came through a break in the purple mass of storm clouds behind me. All this is overdone, I know. I am rambling and wordy simply because I am not enough of a poet to distill into essence of language the dramatic multiplicities of form and color that spread before me in the magic light of waning day. Let me simply say that it was the best view I have ever seen.

*View from Aguereberry Point*

And now to the point of all this prolixity. Why had a road been built to this remote and formerly inaccessible point? *The Monument Guide* says, "Phil Townsend Hanna, an early editor of *Westways*, named this lookout in honor of Pete Aguereberry, a prospector who built a road from his mine to the Point so that others could share his enjoyment of the impressive panorama of Death Valley." How simply it is said: "Built a road." But the days and months of muscle-cracking toil with pick and shovel, the long unpaid hours taken from the more profitable work of mining, the esthetic appreciation that was the seed of the deed, the rare benevolence that wanted to share visual riches—all these lie behind those three words, "Built a road." We know that often rich, philanthropic men endow theaters and libraries, that the J. Paul Gettys and Huntington Hartfords and Norton Simons and J. P. Morgans of this world make rare treasures available to others. But a bewhiskered, bent-backed, hard-handed grubber for gold, a prospector who died poor as did his partner, Shorty Harris, another wanderer of the perilous wastelands—such a man to be named with multi-millionaires, princes, and the affluent and generous mighty, such a man a modern Maecenas? I say "Yes," he ranks with them; perhaps all things considered, above them, and so I give him the title, "Pete Aguereberry, Patron of the Arts."

And now, for sermonic point, I ask a blunt question. "What have *you* done to make life beautiful for others? In what way do you follow the example of that little-known miner and friend of man?"

Let us begin our exposition by a brief definition of beauty, an admittedly hard word to define. According to *Webster's Unabridged*, beauty is "physical response or charm to the senses, originally the sense of sight: grace or fitness exciting keen intellectual or moral pleasure." The esthetics of beauty are exceedingly complicated, and one sentence on that theme is enough. "Beauty is perfection in the sensuous order, and by extension, in the spiritual: that which excites pleasure or admiration for itself rather than for its uses." Briefly, as the poet has said, "Beauty is its own excuse for being." And most of us would concur with the proverb, "Beauty is in the eye of the beholder." In the relationship of men and women, we not infrequently wonder just what a woman sees in a particular man, or he in her. It could be argued either way—love is blind, or else very perceptive. I shun such argument when beauty is linked to the erotic drive. I suppose that even a hippopotamus must at certain seasons be beautiful to another hippopotamus. Our discussion of beauty could be long, but this is certain, that some people are more alive to it than others, and some have a skill to create beauty which lesser folk lack. The artist, in whatever medium he works, be it words, notes, colors, or lines, is a man apart from ordinary men, and must be judged by other rules.

But I want to talk with you in a simpler vein this morning, basing our thinking on such clichés as the facts: that there is beauty, that it has many forms, and that life is not complete without it. I am reminded of my wife's morose comment on an old TV show, "Life can be beautiful, but seldom is." There are three major classical values—truth, beauty, and goodness. Religion is commonly more concerned with truth and goodness than with beauty, but I think that few will quarrel with my contention that life is neither good nor full if it has no quality of beauty, and I hold that I am urging you to a worthy work when I say that it is a high duty of each of us somehow to make life more beautiful for others.

And to leave theory and move into the area of practical ethics, I suggest that we think of beauty in three ways—esthetic, functional, and spiritual—and consider means by which we can interweave these elements into service for others, and thus walk in the footsteps of Pete Aguereberry. I think that many of us, especially women, do recognize the need in life for sheer beauty, the kind that is its own excuse for being. There is a deep hunger for loveliness in humankind, and we all recognize the wisdom of the Persian poet who said, "If I had two loaves of bread I would sell one of them and buy hyacinths to feed my soul." Women have an instinctive appreciation of the worth of beauty. I cravenly skip the matter of the time and money they spend in beauty parlors, since I am not able to trace with competence the fine line of demarcation between how much of this beatification is done for narcissistic reasons and how much is done to bring beauty into the lives of others, which is the principal point of this discourse. But certainly the amount of feminine attention and toil given to the adornment of the home is largely for others, even though there is an indubitable bit of self-satisfaction in such labor. For no house is complete with simply the functions of shelter and warmth and cooking and disposal. Bare walls, roof, hearth, and pail would take care of those necessities. There must be carpets, pictures, flowers, rich upholstery, drapes, bric-a-brac, to give charm. But there are also men who toil so that others may have joy of vision. On 80th Street in Westchester, there is a stunning bank of flowers of many sorts, red, orange, pink, purple, and white, all against emerald, a shouting luxuriance of color. It edges the property of Howard Hughes. (How sad and ironic it is that this self-focussed, enormously wealthy man died of addiction and starvation!) But a man who lives across the street has sown seeds and tended the plants so that on sunshiny spring mornings those who drive down this side street pass a living bouquet a hundred yards long and nine feet wide. He, too, is a lesser patron of the arts and does not even have the satisfaction of a public name, nor do the neighbors that have aided him. I confess with shame that I enjoyed that spectacle for twenty springs and never said thanks. That omission ought to be corrected.

Let us now speak of the beauty of *function*. On a physical level we see it often. At night, when my Abyssinian cat, Robert Browne, goes out for a walk with me, I note with joy the superb articulation of his joints, how muscles ripple under his glossy brown pelt, and how the moon sometimes lights a cold green fire in his eyes. What of the blurred-wing hovering of the ruby-throated humming bird, or the effortless soaring elevations of noble ballet dancers? I cannot wholly approve of the current use of "beautiful" as an ejaculation over a good happening, but I am sure that there are some who properly cry that word when that marvel of athletic precision, the double play, is executed (especially by the Dodgers!). Have you ever noted the exquisite grace and speed of those agile giants, professional football players, when seen in slow motion replays? Well, what I am saying here is that smooth economical function is itself a thing of beauty. I once defined dancing as the art of moving well, and, by extension, life is something of the sort. How well do you move through life? Do you handle hard situations with kindness and lack of fuss? If you do, you are putting a touch of beauty into the lives of those who watch you. I object with heat to the name that has been applied to the ultra-wealthy, transiently famous jetsetters whose names crowd the scandal sheets. They are called "the Beautiful People." They don't deserve it. Their patterns of behavior (Joy Haber's salacious novel of a few years ago, *The Users*, portrays them accurately) are far from beautiful; they are often ugly and meretricious. There is to my mind a greater beauty of function in a father working hard, productively, and unselfishly to give his children a better life than he had, or a woman accomplishing the complex task of mother and homemaker, or some unsung Iphigenia living a life of sacrifice for her parents, than is to be seen in the glittering partyings and migrations of the over-rich and under-worked.

There are, then, beauties of esthetics, function, and the spirit, but the greatest of these is spiritual. Scripture bids us to "worship the Lord in the beauty of holiness." This we find easy to do in a great Gothic sanctuary like First Church, with skying arches, a spacious chancel furnished with wood most excellently carved, God-praising organs and voices, windows that in the morning sun throw blurred prismatic splashes on the transept walls and at evening kindle funeral flames for the day's death; it is also easy in the quieter loveliness of this very room, warm with brown oak, the soft red of brick, and the gold accent of our chancel text, all subtly colored with rich and significant memories. Our Scripture lesson told us of the beauty of the new Jerusalem, the Holy City above, where the redeemed worship, with gates of purest gold and a multilithic splendor of stones in its walls. Scripture also tells us that "The king's daughter is all glorious within" and there are many daughters of Christ the King, no longer young, whose faces shine with an interior light that blesses the eyes of those who look on them and love them. The good people of either sex and all ages who love God and keep his commandments are jewels that richly adorn his doctrine. And I speak of Jesus and his beauty, he who, as the hymn says, was born in "the beauty of the lilies." We do not know the details of his physical appearance; those who wrote of him thought to see him coming soon in a heavenly glory, and so held the shaping of his flesh to be unnecessary to record. But we know that when he took three disciples up into "a high mountain apart, he was transfigured before them, and his face did shine as the sun, and his raiment was white as the light." The hymn of yesterday hailed him as "The lily of the valley,/ The bright and morning star," and our own day sings of fairest Lord Jesus, and we know that while

> Fair is the sunshine
> Fairer still the moonlight
> And all the twinkling starry host:
>
> Jesus shines brighter, Jesus shines purer
> Than all the angels heaven can boast.

Often do sermons speak of Christ's goodness, and of the truth of his words. Insufficiently does the pulpit hail the loveliness of his life, a life that reflects beauty into the drab or dark or ugly lives of those who love him and seek to follow him. Jesus is the supreme patron of the arts of the soul. We ought to follow his example, and live and work like him and the prospector of the Panamints so that the lives of others will have an added touch of beauty because we have passed this way before them.
—*Congregational Church of the Messiah, 1981.*

## 25

## The Long, Cold Night on Mt. McDill

> And when Pharaoh drew nigh, the children of Israel lifted up their eyes, and, behold the Egyptians marched after them, and they were sore afraid . . . and they said to Moses, because there were no graves in Egypt, hast thou taken us away to die in the wilderness?
>
> Exodus 14:10, 14

Shortly after I purchased my present pickup truck, I was seized with an understandable desire to get out on a steep and rocky way to test its capabilities. I didn't have time to go deep into the back country, so, one pleasant fall day, I set out for the near-at-hand Sierra Pelona area. I cruised up Bouquet Canyon and just past the reservoir, turned south on the Artesian Springs Road. It was good comfortable climbing past Willow Springs and the road to Sierra Pelona Lookout where, on occasion, the winds rage mightily. Then I began to hit steeper grades and ruttier roads and I rejoiced that my new toy had such power. At last I came to a locked gate which barred the road to the summit of Mt. McDill. It was getting late, and I didn't want the long retracing of my route. So I decided to investigate a doubtful looking trail which went steeply down the mountainside to Lincoln Crest on the paved road. But before I had gone a hundred yards, and saw the scars of a battle between a four-wheel-drive and the now nearly 40 degree trail. That was too much for me, so I went back, and started homeward. I couldn't move in reverse; too slippery. I got out, not perturbed, and put my two rubber mats which I carry for this express purpose, under the rear wheels. The tires simply spit them forward, and

I gained a foot. I started to get worried, and after winding up the tach until there was a troublesome smell of hot rubber and overworked clutch, I found I had made about three feet up the hill. Dry grass offers little more traction than ice.

Now I really began to worry. It was getting late in the October afternoon and I was at an altitude of 5000 feet wearing only a light sweater. In my old truck (and in this new one now) I have all sorts of cold weather gear, but this one then was new and unequipped. Unexpectedly, my maiden voyage with my powerful new vehicle showed every indication of becoming a long, cold night on Mt. McDill. I couldn't walk the twenty miles back to Saugus. I sat down and thought. On the other side of the trail was a brief opening in the scrub. I figured that if I could swing into that, I might launch a new assault on the twenty-five yards of steepness that stood between me and escape. I loaded my tonneau with several hundred pounds of big rocks; the cruel scars are still there to this day. This, I figured, would give me traction. I opened her up, surged backwards onto the road, holding the front wheels in as tight a cut as I could. I made ten yards, and started to spin. Off to the left, a little above the first opening, I saw another, and going into low, I went shooting off into the bushes and stopped. I walked ahead a way and saw that if I could get traction I could grind through the brush and dodge the big boulders, and I might regain the road above the steep grade. I offered up a brief prayer, a Lord-be-merciful-to-me-a-fool sort of orison, and started forward. The weight on the rear wheels, plus the backward slope of the vehicle, caused the tires to bite and, in less than a minute, I was back on navigable road. Shaking with reaction, I crawled out. It was months before my clutch worked smoothly again. But I had escaped a freezing night, which to one of my poor resistance to chill, could have easily resulted in hypothermia.

Now at this point it is quite possible that some listener is saying, "What has this rambling introduction to do with the title of this piece? It is named 'The Long, Cold Night on Mt. McDill,' and it is apparent that no such nocturnal alpine frigidity took place. What's the point?" The point, to begin with, is that things which don't happen are often important. I am a Sherlock Holmes buff, and I consider that one of the delightful passages in Conan Doyle's inimitable mysteries occurs in *The Adventure of Silver Blaze*. An attempt to tamper with a race horse brings the archetypal detective onto the scene.

After examination of the premises, Dr. Watson asks, "Is there any point to which you would wish to draw my attention?"

"To the curious incident of the dog in the night time."

"The dog did nothing in the night time."

"That was the curious incident," remarked Sherlock Holmes.

The point of this rather famous quotation is that since the dog did not bark, the perpetrator of the crime must have been one friendly with him, which greatly narrowed the field of suspects and led to the solution of the mystery.

I now call your attention to the bad things that we fear which never come to pass. I deal with the point made by the sage who said, "I am an old man, and have seen much trouble, most of which never happened." Now the usual reaction to this philosophy is that we are foolish to worry about the evils that threaten but never eventuate. My thesis will be that, far from dismissing these malign foreshadowings as detrimental, we should realize that these negations can have a positive value in our living. I might well have named this discourse "In Praise of Apprehensiveness" or, perhaps, "The Value of Fear." To live the full life we must not constantly run scared, but it is only the fool who never runs scared.

The worth of fear is too much minimized in our culture. We are constantly urging children not to be afraid. We tend to avoid those realistic old fairy tales which are full of ogres and witches and wolves and divers inimical monsters because a school of child care holds that fear cramps and warps the personality. In point of fact, for the infinitely vast majority of living creatures, fear is a continual fact of life, and, I hold, at times a beneficial emotion. It is quite true, as Thomas Hobbes morosely observed, that primitive man had no easy time of it, "No arts, no science, no navigation, and worst of all continual fear, and the life of man in a state of nature, nasty, poor, brutish, and short." But it is the man's or animal's continual fear, in a hostile environment, that keeps him alive.

The animal without apprehension is soon trapped, killed, or eaten. Unfortunately, in our time, the world out there is becoming more and more like the jungle, in which beasts roam to prey on the helpless and the desirable. Holdups, rape, and random murder are making our streets as perilous as ever jungle was. But even in safer situations, where armed enemies are absent, there is still a value in the apprehension that is born of fear. In the most ordered life there is a place for apprehension. To live in blissful unconcern, being neither aware of nor afraid of, the brutal exigencies of life, is to be a simpleton. Most of us have some awareness of this, and that is why we buy insurance policies and have savings accounts. We often pay considerable sums, to our annoyance, for protection against the long, cold nights on Mt. McDill that never take place, but few of us fail to make such plans for possible disaster. We are apprehensive about sickness and bad breaks, and loss of jobs, and we exercise a prudent foresight.

I now make two points in favor of fear; the first is that fear is an innovator, or more precisely, a force for innovation. When we are thrust into a fear-arousing situation, we are stimulated to find ways out of the trouble. To be sure, blind fear—panic—can inhibit and paralyze us. But if we are reasonably strong people, of stout heart, fear moves us to do things we have never previously done before. A trivial example: I had never before put a load of rocks in my car to gain traction; the apprehension of the night of cold moved me to do so. Fear was the mother of invention. A more serious case: When the Bennett-Arcane party was escaping from Death Valley after their gruelling ordeal at Piaute Springs, they came into Butte Valley and went down what is now known as Redlands Canyon. Suddenly they came to a twenty-foot drop, a sheer cliff impassable by wagon. The fear of death by privation was still with them, and it was a stimulus to innovation. They took their wagons apart, and lowered them piece by piece to the foot of the cliff, where they were laboriously reassembled.

One of the mighty innovations of all human development came sometime in the mists of prehistory. Mankind then was nomadic, depending for food upon the grass of the steppes and the hard-to-get flesh of wild beasts. Someone (James Michener suggests it was a woman), prodded by the fear of starvation, tended a few shoots of wild grain by a spring. In a few years she created the first farm, and at that pivotal moment in time, man ceased to be a nomad and hunter; he started to till the soil; agrarian culture was born, and because of that shift, that strange thing called the city came into being. Well, fear does not always produce such immense results, but when you are scared, really afraid of losing something, or of a wicked threat, you have found yourself coming up with new ideas or attitudes or innovations which would never have been put into operation in time of fear-free ease.

In the second place, fear is the energizer. It not only stimulates the mind, but it gives strength to the body. The common dramatic example is that of the 110 pound mother, who, fearing for the life of her child, pinned down by 3000 pounds of overturned automobile, lifts one end of the car off the child. Chased across a Maine pasture by a crazy, murderous cow, I once cleared a five-strand barbed wire fence, a feat quite beyond my normal leaping ability. Fear is a built-in biological preserver or life. Fear and pain are things we try to avoid, and yet both are, in a deep sense, friendly things. Pain is a signal; it tells us something is wrong; it sends us to the doctor or to remedial action. Fear starts the adrenalin pumping. The sudden pulse-jump, the quick breath, the sweating palms, are all lubricants to the motor of the body which must instantly be ready for tremendous exertions of escape or battle. Now, because we live in situations where physical flight or combat is not the solution to situations of social or psychological peril, this biological device for triggering great motor response can backfire. Our bodies, having become racing engines generating physical power, are helpless when the peril is financial or legal or social. Fear as mere physical energizer can become an inhibitor, a paralyzing force, making us immobile or impotent. Fear is like nitroglycerin, a cardiac lifesaver or shattering explosive.

Now then, to the practical point of this discourse. How can we avoid or lessen those disturbing apprehensions of evil things to come? All of us know those troubled days and nights when we face a bad tomorrow— a confrontation we must make, an appointment of great potential grief, a word of decision which might change life for the worse? Perhaps these baleful things may never come to pass; they are long, cold nights on Mt. McDill; or they may prove to be authentic griefs and disasters. In any event, they cast their dark shadows before them, and we know fear. How face that fear? Let us look to Scripture for an answer. We find one in our text. Behind them the people of Israel saw the oncoming hosts of Pharaoh, before them was the impassable Red Sea, "and they were sore afraid, and they said unto Moses, because there were no graves in Egypt, hast thou taken us away to die in this wilderness?" Moses' answer was a superb affirmation of faith, "Fear ye not: stand still, and see the salvation of the Lord . . . and Moses stretched out his hand over the sea, and the Lord caused the sea to go back . . . and the children of Israel went into the sea on dry ground."

It was not their own strength that saved them, but the Lord's; not in their own doing lay salvation, but in God's work. The fear that seized the Jews was spawned of ignorance and unfaith; they did not know they were God's children, his chosen people, and they did not believe in his power to save. Sonorous clichés, these, but their redeeming worth is that they are true. And lest we condemn these terrified fugitives for their cravenness, let us think of how like them we often are. We, too, are God's children; he has concern and care for each of us. But in darkness of premonition we forget this, and the candle of our faith goes out at three o'clock in the morning before the dark day. A simple and sovereign cure for the sickness of fear when trouble looms is to realize that God is with you, "The Lord is my light and my salvation; whom shall I fear? The Lord is the light of my life, of whom shall I be afraid?" "The Lord is on my side, I will not fear: what can man do unto me?" For the man and woman of faith, these ancient cries are trumphet sounds before battle; villains, dragons, and goblins flee at their sound.

Jesus deals with the problem of the dark tomorrow, the long, cold night that is never suffered, or the actual impact of disaster. He puts his core thought in lucid language. "Take therefore no thought for the morrow: for the morrow shall take thought for the things of itself: sufficient unto the day is the evil thereof." The fifty-seven scholars who worked for King James wrote lovely lines, but occasionally they faltered. The Greek word they translated as "take no thought"—*merimrao*—means literally "to be anxious, to be troubled with cares." Jesus does not tell us to lack foresight, to make no plans for the day ahead. What he literally says is, "Don't worry about tomorrow." And why not worry about the bill you can't pay, the interview you dread, the words you must say or hear? Because you have a heavenly Father, Jesus tell us, and he will care for you as he cares for the birds of the air and the lilies of the field; he cares even more, for you are better than they. This is the certainty of faith that enables the believer to be ready in soul for whatever tomorrow brings.

There is a relevant passage in *Hamlet* where the dark-starred prince, just before his fatal duel with Laertes, is talking with his friend Horatio. Hamlet knows he is a better swordsman than Laertes, but he also knows a troublesome misgiving. He touches his breast and says, "But thou wouldst not think how ill all's here about my heart." But when Horatio would postpone the duel, Hamlet forbids him in those oft-quoted words which bespeak the code of the brave natural man in the presence of imminent peril. "If it be now, 'tis not to come; if it be not to come, it will be now; if it be not now, yet it will come. The readiness is all."

True, true. But how do we get that readiness? How can we face with equanimity the long, cold night on Mt. McDill, the trouble that never happens, but is terribly possible? For me, and for other believers, there is a simple, almost naive, but unfailingly sustaining cast of soul; I believe that I am a child of God, and that whether the morrow be stormy or fair, I am in his keeping. Tomorrow, bright or dark, sweet or bitter, is not a thing of our making alone, nor the whim of capricious fate; God is the Lord of tomorrow, as he is of all time, and of eternity. Believe that he is the determiner of your destiny, your caring Heavenly Father, and you will face the unknown future, not without trepidation, but with assurance. The Book tells us that Jesus knew agony and unwillingness in Gethsemane in the face of an evil Friday, but his incomparable faith in his Father's care sustained him during the long, cold night in the tomb that ended at the world's supreme sunrise.

Take this thought to the Table.

—*First Congregational Church of Los Angeles, 1983.*

# 26

# The Mayor of Corn Springs: La Dolce Vita

> For what is your life?
> *James 4:14b*

On a pleasant afternoon last November I was driving along Route 10 on my way to a speaking engagement in Sun City, Arizona. In relatively strange territory I like to try little travelled back roads, and so, some ten miles east of Desert Center, I turned south at the Corn Springs Exit and headed up the wash. It was easy driving and shortly I found myself at Corn Springs, a place of huge tumbled rocks, tall palms, and no water. I had the place to myself (which I liked) and I spent an uneventful night. In the morning I pushed up the wash a few miles to Aztec Springs, where the road suddenly changed to a jeep trail too tough for Excelsior, my little truck. On the way back I caught a glimpse of a greenish bronze plaque, half hidden by foliage, which I had missed on the way in. The inscription said that until 1920, when the springs inexplicably dried up, a number of prospectors made this their center. The place became a ghost town, but, the inscription continued, "One prospector, Gus Lederer, settled down, built a cabin, grew vegetables, and helped travellers. He became known as the Mayor of Corn Springs." "Ha," I muttered, "this is the stuff of sermons." Out came my notebook, and words and date were jotted down for later elaboration, which now takes place.

Consider with me the theme of the good life. It has many forms, and I shall maintain that Gus Lederer's was certainly one of them. But I would be less than realistic if I did not recognize that the common idea of the good life is certainly not that which the Mayor of Corn Springs led in his desert home. Perhaps some of you saw, twenty odd years ago, Frederico Fellini's movie masterpiece, "La Dolce Vita"—the sweet life. It was a brilliant treatment of life among the Roman aristocracy. These people had wealth, social position, power, and beauty. The picture was a staggering depiction of their decadence, corruption, and hopelessness. The title was, of course, ironic; it captured a story of life without honor, fidelity, ideals, love, or strength of spirit. But, curiously, there are many people in this metropolis, perhaps the majority, who would think that the pleasures and perquisites which are possessed by today's equivalent of the depraved Romans—that is, the Jet Set, the beautiful people of the entertainment world in Hollywood and Vegas, in London, Paris, West Berlin—truly are the factors of the good life. Money, power, frequent mention by columnists, membership in an in-group, easy sex and available cocaine, being where the action is, these things, many think, with envy, are the essentials of "la dolce vita," the sweet life, the good life. For them, Corn Springs would be an earthly hell.

Further, a great number of less high-style people (my wife would be one such) would hold that life at Corn Springs, with its heat and isolation, would by no means be a good life; they would go mad out there. Even I, who know more about the Mojave than most, find the cliché applicable: the desert is a nice place to visit, but I wouldn't want to live there. Now Gus Lederer lived in another time, another world, a simpler time, a simpler world. Absent were the miracles of transportation and communication we take for granted. True, the movies were starting to change the mores of America, radio enthusiasts were huddling over their crystal sets, but it would be a few years before the first presidential election returns were sent out from KDKA in Pittsburgh. The party line phone was an institution, but TV was a thing of tomorrow and our latest technical craze, the computer, was not yet a beautiful gleam in Norbert Wiener's eye. Ours is a more complex world; we would find it hard to live in Corn Springs, no TV, no car, no supermarket, and it was a long hot ride to Indio or Blythe to get flour and bacon and sugar and coffee. But these lacks stated, I am going to maintain that it was possible for a good life to be lived in such barrenness, and that Gus Lederer lived one.

To begin with, the very sparseness and simplicity of life at Corn Springs was a condition wise men have sought. The early Christians fled to the Thebaid, the Egyptian desert, to escape the corruptions of a society in decay. And that American sage, H. D. Thoreau, went to the woods by Walden Pond to seek what Gus Lederer had, a life stripped to its essentials. "Simplicity, simplicity, simplicity," Henry cried, "let your affairs be as two or three, and not a hundred or a thousand; instead of a million, count half a dozen, and keep your accounts on your thumbnail ... Simplify, simplify. Instead of three meals a day, if necessary eat one." And as to the technology which is in full evil bloom today, he would say of it what he said of the telegraph and the railroad, that superb phase of dismissal, "improved means to unimproved ends." So Gus lived long with what Henry briefly know, and indeed I doubt if Henry could have stood the harshness of life at Corn Springs, for at Walden his nearest neighbor was but a mile away and his sister could walk over from Concord on a pleasant afternoon bringing him freshly baked cookies. In the second place, Gus was doing what he wanted to do. This life, austere and isolated, was of his choosing. He might have packed up and gone with the others as the springs dwindled, but he elected to remain, independent, as free as mortal man can be free. He was, like Robinson Crusoe,

>The monarch of all he surveyed:
>His right there was none to dispute.

And we who fret under the orders of bosses, the pressures of our peers, the stress of family living, lack something which independent Gus had.

But these are generalities; let's look at the text of the inscription, for in terse language it states the core of his deeds. "He settled down," says the plaque. Now "settling down" is a complex operation, mingled, of several colors. For there is a sense in which every man or woman is a pilgrim, a traveller; he has a desired haven, a goal—"miles to go before he sleeps." It is a high virtue of youth that the young want to be moving on and out, to leave the old home town, to get ahead, to be upwardly mobile. But there comes a time when mobility is no longer the prime virtue; a mature person must have an abiding place, even though it be but a stage or rest in the eternal journey of the soul. There is a difference between a pilgrim and a tramp: the pilgrim has a celestial city; the tramp wanders without destination and dies en route, never having stopped long enough to leave his mark on any place or on any people. Gus Lederer ceased his wanderings in the Chuckwallas, Eagle, Coxcomb, and the Palen Mountains—the blistering heat, the dry water holes, the runaway burros, the sand storms, the unprofitable lodes and the glory hole that was never found—and came to a place of quiet and rest. So may we all do when our big work is over, our ambitions satisfied, and our flesh weary of wandering.

It is written, "He built a cabin." No more the chance-found cave, the clump of cottonwood trees, the blankets under the stars. Gus raised a roof over his head and stout walls against the wind. But we must not meagerly misconstrue this clause as a mere matter of housing; the act has spiritual overtones. For there comes to mind a group of desert wanderers of long ago, who spent forty years in a bleak and hostile wilderness, and many more in fighting their way to the promised land. During these centuries-long peregrinations they carried with them the Ark of the Lord, a tabernacle; dare I say God in a box? But there came a day when they settled down and under David made a holy city, and under Solomon erected a temple for God, a stately house that was patterned after that house not made with hands, eternal in the heavens. And when Israel settled down and built a house they began that interior journey of spiritual exploration that culminated in the birth, life, death and resurrection of Jesus Christ. Philosophy did not begin among the Greeks until men had leisure to think. The Jews grew in spiritual power when they had a house in which they could read their great book.

It is further written that "He grew vegetables." With the residual water from the once free-flowing springs Gus followed God's early example, for we read that "the Lord God planted a garden eastward in Eden, and there he put the man that he had formed." Not until there was a garden was the world fit for man to live in. And lest I be tempted to soar into theological panegyrics on the meaning of the Garden of Eden I speak of more earthy matters. High up in the Panamint Mountains there is a ghost town called Panamint City (bad road-fate has thrice thwarted my efforts to get there), and one day, a hundred odd years ago, the editor of the short-lived newspaper lamented that "green vegetables are scarce. A good head of cabbage would bring two dollars." And on the other side of the range crest an enterprising group of Swiss immigrants planted gardens and took their produce by burros into hungry Panamint City. It is said that the older orchards still survive high in the hills. Gus's garden not only has the grandest of spiritual precedents, but it met a basic human need. And I find it curious that one of the efforts of this unlettered prospector turned farmer carried out what one of the world's most sophisticated minds said was the true duty and only wise employment of the civilized man. You may remember Voltaire's classic work *Candide*, from your college days, and you may also remember what the philosopher, sage Dr. Pangloss decided was the only reasonable employment of a wise man: "I cultivate my garden."

It is further written of Gus Lederer, that "He aided travellers." To this point his achievements are self-centered; here he expands into altruism. When I was a boy I committed to memory Sam Walter Foss' poem, "The House by the Side of the Road." As I stood by the plaque at Corn Springs I read aloud portions of that verse from the faded photographic memory plate in the back of my mind.

> There are hermit souls that live withdrawn
> In the peace of their self-content;
> There are souls, like stars, that dwell apart,

In a fellowless firmament;
There are pioneer souls that blaze their paths
Where highways never ran;
But let me live by the side of the road
And be a friend to man.

Let me live in my house by the side of the road
Where the race of men go by—
They are good, they are bad, they are weak, they are strong,
Wise, foolish—so am I.
Then why should I sit in the scorner's seat
Or hurl the cynic's ban?—
Let me live in my house by the side of the road
And be a friend to man.

Now the Somerville librarian acknowledges his debt to Homer, who writes of a Greek hero: "He was a friend to man, and lived in a house by the side of the road." But in Gus Lederer's friendship we find echoes of a tale told by one greater than Homer, Christ's immortal story of the good Samaritan, who, though he did not live in a house on the Jericho Road, nevertheless was a friend to the poor traveller who fell among thieves and was robbed, beaten, and left for dead. That Samaritan, said Christ, obeyed the second half of the Great Commandment and loved his neighbor as himself. He then turned to the truth-seeking lawyer and said, "Go, and do thou likewise." It was not an injunction for that one man; Christ lays upon each of us his disciples an imperative to help the needy, to show mercy, to care for those in trouble, in short, to be a friend to man. Otherwise, we cannot be friends with God, nor will he be to us.

The final bronze word tells us that Gus Lederer became known as "The Mayor of Corn Springs." No life is complete without some meed of honor, be it small or great. I once read an apothegm by some cracker box philosopher: "It's a poor man that ain't king in some small corner." Every man or woman of reasonable ego (and not to have an ego is not to be a person) wants recognition. Perhaps not a grand title, but acknowledgement of work done well. We are willing to work without constant praise or frequent raises in salary, but when work is over we need the stated respect and honor of those around us; life has a bitter taste else. To be "The Mayor of Corn Springs" has a flavor of humor, since it may well be that the Mayor himself was the only inhabitant of that oasis. But I am sure that the humor was warm, and those weary and thirsty wanderers through the desert sands did not use the title "Mayor" in derision.

It was the crowning of an obscure life lived in simplicity and with a concern for others.

Now I confess to you that I am grieved at the conclusion I must make to this sermon. I have said that the life Gus Lederer lived at Corn Springs was a good life. Morally, psychologically, it was an excellent life. But it lacked one thing, and that the most important—God. The deeds and qualities noted in bronze were things of worth, but they are purely humanistic. They touch upon the horizontal aspect of life—the relationship of man to man—but the vertical aspect—the upthrust of man for God and the down-reach of God to man—is missing. Now I must not say with certainty that the element of faith in God was missing in the Mayor of Corn Springs. It is hard to see how a man could dwell in the vastness of the desert, being a living dot in the center of the mountain-ringed spatial majesty, sleep under the cold unceasing fire of the stars, spend his years in a procession of days each curtained by the splendor of dawns and sunsets, without being aware of his Maker and his need for his Maker. I surmise that, like most dwellers in the desert, Gus Lederer believed in God, but I have been dealing with the record, and the record makes no mention of his faith. And in fidelity to the Gospel I must declare that life is not wholly good unless it is God-touched. So Jesus taught; so men and women of faith know. And I say to all who hear me now, that life without God, however rich in earthly contentments it may be, however beautifully simple, is not complete. Life without him can be good, but it cannot be the best. Only if we know him, only if we live with him and in him, can we experience what is truly La Dolce Vita, the sweet life.

—*First Congregational Church of Los Angeles, 1984.*

Many are the ways in which men may live,
Many the times and paths in which they may walk,
Many the cloaks of flesh each spirit may put on,
And many are the means by which the one God can
    bring these as-yet-young souls of ours to
    such strength and maturity as will enable
    us to see His face.
                      *—Harry R. Butman, April 11, 1971.*

# Epilogue

Those who have read thus far are aware that this book has two distinct sections. The first generally deals with the desert as a geographical reality, and in particular telling of certain motorized rambles in the remote environs of North America's most noted desert locale, Death Valley, together with comments on things seen and happenings on the way. The second is simply a book of sermons—a literary form immensely popular in America a century ago, but now not much printed and little read.

But this dichotomy is more seeming than real; there is an underlying unity—the relationship of the vast spatial fact of the desert to the enduring spiritual fact of the desert, a fact, as the prologue noted, which was a major element in shaping the origins and development of the three great religions of the Western world, Judaism, Christianity, and Islam. The desert molded the souls and doctrines of three mighty men of faith, Moses, Jesus, and Muhammad. This book is an attempt to tell how the desert touched the character and thought of a very minor man of religion—me. I went to the desert as Thoreau went to the woods of Walden Pond, not as seriously as he, of course, for I went in part to have fun, while he was driven by a grim Puritan resolve to find the true and whole meaning of life. And I had my fun and found my truth.

I pencilled these concluding words alone in a wash near Yaqui Well in the Anza-Borrego Desert. I wrote under an ash, gray, and bluesilver sunset that only briefly flared into sullen red, and in the windless dusk I found myself wondering why so many people are unaware of the vision of God as he may be seen in the desert, not the least of his wondrous works.

True, man has seen the face of God in nature time out of mind, from the pantheism of ancient India and Greece even until now. But it is the watery element of the cosmos that gets the most attention—rivers, lakes, seas, lush meadows, and noble trees. The poets are eloquent on this point. "The groves were man's first temples," says Bryant. In the brooks and cataracts of the wet Cotswolds Wordsworth found intimations of Deity. Byron apostrophizes the sea:

> Roll on, thou deep and dark blue Ocean—roll!
> ... Thou glorious mirror, where the Almighty's form
> Glasses itself in tempests . . .

And a lesser lyricist sings the superhuman attributes of Old Man River, who, heedless of the brief and bitter years of men, just keeps rolling along. Perhaps the desert is disliked because in the primal order of things, wetness came before dryness; the first land creatures crawled out of the warm shallows onto some primeval beach. Or, if your mind is of Scriptural rather than scientific cast, you remember that Genesis reveals that the watery chaos of the great abyss existed before God made the dry land on the third day. The dryness of the desert repels and frightens. Water is birth and life; dryness is death. The skeleton is dry bones, and all flesh becomes a handful of dust.

But despite these old intimidating fears, some men and women have sought out God in the arid wilderness and found him. God is not limited in his epiphanies. He is to be known in the revelations of sacred books, in the traditions of the Church, in history and the ponderings of philosopher and theologians, in the contemplation of the innumerable circling suns that orbit in deep space, in the closeness of lovers, the trust of children, the mystic's experience, and in a certain short Life in Judea. These visions are varied, not stereotyped copies of the great Original. The God who makes himself known in the immensities and solitudes of the desert does not wear the kindly countenance of a loving heavenly Father: he will not smile. Nikos Kazantzakis tells of "the Cretan glance," the third eye that discovers the inner and hidden things that the right eye and the left cannot see. And there are those who have gone out into the emptiness, the lethal dryness, the shimmering salt flats under the inverted blue bowl of the hot sky—the enormous nonhuman reality—and looked with the third eye and seen the desert face of God.

## Selected References

Abbey, Edward. *Desert Solitaire.* Peregrine Smith, 1968.
Cowles, Raymond B. *Desert Journal.* University of California Press, 1977.
Dodge, Natt N. & Janish, Jeanne R. *Flowers of the Southwest Deserts.* Southwestern Monuments Association, 1969.
Ferris, R. S. *The Flowers of Death Valley.* Death Valley Natural History Association, 1974.
Grey, Zane. *Wanderer of the Wastelands.* Grosset & Dunlap, 1923.
Jaeger, Edmund C. *The California Deserts* (Fourth Edition). Stanford University Press, 1965.
_____. *Desert Wild Flowers* (Revised Edition). Stanford University Press, 1969.
_____. *Desert Wildlife.* Stanford University Press, 1961.
Kirk, Ruth. *Exploring Death Valley* (Third Edition). Stanford University Press, 1981.
Lawrence, T. E. *The Seven Pillars of Wisdom.* Doubleday & Co., 1966.
Melville, Herman. *Moby Dick.* Numerous editions.
Olin, George & Cannon, Jerry. *Mammals of the Southwest Deserts.* Southwestern Monuments Association, 1965.
Paher, Stanley W. *Death Valley Ghost Towns.* Nevada Publications; Vol. I, 1981; Vol. II, 1982.
Sanders, Ed. *The Family: Charles Manson's Dune Buggy Attack Battalion.* Dalton, 1971.
Strong, Mary Francis. *Desert Gem Trails.* Gembooks, 1971.
Thesigner, Wilfrid. *Arabian Sands.* Longman, England, 1959.
Biblical quotes from the King James Version.

# Index

Aguereberry, Pete, 72, 142
Aguereberry Point, 72, 142
Amargosa Road, 18-19, 42, 71
Badwater, 16, 90
Baja California, 44, 95-98
Baker, 18, 42
Ballarat, 25, 26, 48, 122
Bennett-Arcane party, 35, 50, 154
Black Mountain, 103
Burros, 31, 109-110, 113
Butte Valley, 30, 49
Camp sites, 24
   Furnace Creek, 24
   Lee Flat, 28
   Mesquite Springs, 32, 54
   Stovepipe Wells, 15, 24
Cerro Gordo, 29, 70
Cottonwood Canyon, 69
Cowhorn Valley, 22, 33
Crankcase Junction, 22, 36
Dante's View, 16, 72
Death Valley Scotty, 16
Dunes, 34
El Paso Mountains, 103
Emigrant Pass, 129
Eureka Dunes, 34
Goler Wash, 22, 26, 45
Greenwater, 39, 136

Harris, Shorty, 16-18, 26, 122
Inyo Range, 29, 65, 109
Jackass Flat, 29, 30
Kangaroo Rats, 55, 145
Kit fox, 19
Last Chance Range, 22, 35, 63
Lederer, Gus, 157
Leadfield, 71
Lee Flat, 28
Little Sand Spring, 22, 35-36
Manson, Charles, 26, 44-48
Mengel Pass, 45
Myers Ranch, 45, 46, 48
Owens Dry Lake, 70, 71
Panamint, 25, 48, 77, 108-109, 122
Quail, 34
Racetrack, 24, 37, 144, 145
Raven, 35
Rats, 83
Roadrunner, 61
San Lucas Canyon, 28
Saratoga Springs, 12, 69
Scotty's Castle, 16
Teakettle Junction, 37, 145
Titus Canyon, 71
Warm Springs, 32, 45, 51
Waucoba Pass, 22, 31, 32, 33